I0825518

NO FINISH LINE

A RACER'S JOURNEY OF PASSION, PERSEVERANCE, AND PURPOSE

SAM SCHMIDT

WITH **DON YAEGER**

DIVERSION BOOKS

Diversion Books
A division of Diversion Publishing Corp.
www.diversionbooks.com

For more information, email info@diversionbooks.com

First Diversion Books Edition: May 2026
Hardcover ISBN: 9798895151617
e-ISBN: 9798895151624
Design by Westchester Publishing Services
Cover design by Tom Lau
Project Directors Savannah Schmidt Boehrer and Dr. Kimberly Meesters
Photos provided by Arrow Electronics, IMS Photo, and Braedon Flynn

Printed in the United States of America
3 5 7 9 10 8 6 4 2

This book is dedicated to:

My parents, Marv and Judy
They built the road map with their relentless work ethic, rock-solid faith, and unwavering commitment to their marriage vows. I am blessed to have that type of example as my North Star, and I strive every day to live up to it.

My wife, Sheila
This example would mean nothing without someone strong enough to support me through this journey. She carried the weight of every hard day and celebrated every good one. This book exists because she believed I still had more life to live.

CONTENTS

THE FINE PRINT

THIS BOOK is a work of nonfiction based on my personal memories, experiences, and perspectives. While every effort has been made to present events and conversations accurately, some details have been altered for narrative clarity.

The medical episodes in this book are personal recollections and not professional assessments of medical care. Readers should not rely on any medical or health-related information in these pages as a substitute for consultation with qualified medical professionals.

INTRODUCTION

ON JANUARY 6, 2000, Sam Schmidt, the promising racecar driver who had just won his first Indy Racing League competition in his adopted hometown of Las Vegas, Nevada, backed into a wall at the Walt Disney World Speedway in Orlando, Florida. He did so at around two hundred miles per hour and, as a result, Sam broke his neck. He was quickly airlifted to Orlando Regional Medical Center before being transferred to Barnes-Jewish Hospital in St. Louis, Missouri, where he spent six months in rehabilitation before going home to his new life with his loving wife, Sheila, and their two young children, Savannah and Spencer.

For over twenty-six years, Sam has learned to live paralyzed. But being a quadriplegic has not slowed him down. Almost immediately after his accident, he started a foundation that has raised millions of dollars for spinal cord injury research and rehabilitation. He founded a racing team that's won many races and championships. He's driven cars again thanks to cutting-edge technology. His children have grown. He spoke at his son's college graduation and danced on two legs with his daughter at her wedding. Sam's philosophy is, you either get busy doing the work or you get busy waiting to die. For him, the latter is not an option.

In October 2024, Sam's foundation opened its newest DRIVEN facility in Indianapolis, Indiana, which offers people with spinal cord injuries and other neurological disorders the chance to rehab when their insurance policies (or lack thereof) won't allow it. He has become a paragon of hope and remains a pillar in the racing community. Indeed, Sam says he has done much more after (and because of) his accident than he would have otherwise. A former control freak, he has learned to delegate. A once-singularly-minded, self-described egocentric racer, he now lives to help others. The son of a driver who was also paralyzed from the sport, Sam has lived an astonishing, driven life . . . and there is no finish line in sight.

This is his journey.

—Don Yaeger
2026

1

A FATHER'S DREAM

EVERY DAD of a little girl dreams of the day he will walk his daughter down the aisle. I did. Then came the crash. When I woke up from my racing accident in 2000, the first thing I felt wasn't pain; it was loss. Loss of that dream and of every moment I had pictured for her future and mine.

Paralyzed . . . My entire body was paralyzed, and the doctor resolutely said I would never breathe on my own, let alone ever walk my daughter down the aisle. Thankfully, she was only a toddler, and time was on our side. I knew I had to fight. Whether it was the mindset of a professional athlete or the resilience my parents had instilled in me, I pushed back every negative thought. I made a decision that day, that I continue to make every day, that I would choose to find purpose and hope in my situation by focusing on meaningful goals.

Thankfully, with the help of incredible people along the way, I have spent the last twenty-six years accomplishing many of those goals. I started a foundation to support people in my situation, built successful Indy Lights and IndyCar teams, became the first high-level quadriplegic to get a driver's license, and worked to change the way people think about paralysis and other neurological conditions. While I am incredibly proud of these purposeful endeavors, nothing has meant more than when I stood, for the first time in twenty-one years and danced with my daughter on her wedding day. You read that correctly; I actually did it. I stood on my own two feet and danced with my beautiful daughter, Savannah, on April 25, 2021, the day she married her husband, Adam.

Before we get into the events that took place and the technological breakthroughs that led to the momentous occasion, let me take a step back. My accident happened on January 6, 2000, at Walt

Disney World Speedway. Sheila and I had been married for seven years. Savannah was just two and a half years old and my son, Spencer, was only six months old. Neither child has any memory of a hug from me. Savannah's first memories were of my hospital room. They don't remember me ever standing, and I have to assume Savannah never thought I would walk her down the aisle. A dream like that was so far out of reach. The kids never really had to adjust to our lifestyle because it was their *normal* from the beginning of their lives. We learned to move through the world in our own rhythm, quietly accommodating the details that made our family unique.

Every once in a while, life would hand us a reminder that our version of "normal" wasn't quite like everyone else's. One of those moments came when we found ourselves trying to navigate something as seemingly ordinary as a father-daughter middle school dance. When Savannah was in sixth grade, we made it a point to say we'd go to the dance together. In the back of both of our minds, though, we weren't sure how it was going to work. How do you dance with someone in a wheelchair? We'd moved back and forth to music before, but it was never anything *formal*. As the day approached, the idea of dancing together in front of her classmates was becoming overwhelming for her. I was away on a trip and returned home on the day of the dance. We hadn't really talked about how we'd handle the dancing part. When I got home, Sheila said Savannah was "sick" and I knew exactly what she meant. That night, I played along, even though it hurt that we couldn't go. We didn't talk about it after that. Then years later she finally confessed she was so nervous that she pretended to be sick that day just to avoid going. Savannah says that back then our philosophy was that you either make the thing work, and it feels normal, or you don't talk about it at all. There was no middle ground. She was right. During their childhoods, it felt impossible to discuss those moments in our lives that just couldn't be "normal."

When we took the kids to Disneyland, strangers approached us to tell me they had followed my career, including the accident, and that I inspired them. "It's great to meet you, buddy!" they'd say. "I can't believe you're here!" And when we were at the racetrack . . . Forget about it. I'd be swarmed by racers, fans, and everyone in between. My kids have told me that they felt important just standing next to me at the track. Back home, it was harder. I traveled a lot for work, and I think the fact that I was away so many days of the year made it easier for the kids. They didn't have to think about their father being wheelchair-bound. How he was different from all the other dads. At least that is what I told myself.

The hardest moments for me were those where it felt like I was missing out on being a dad. The middle school dance was just one example of many. I could not drive them to school, play with them on the floor, or teach them to drive a stick shift. I couldn't even tuck them in at night. We were so lucky to be able to convert the downstairs to be accessible for me, but the kids' bedrooms were still upstairs.

Even as I grieved what I couldn't do, I found new ways to show up. I learned to be part of their world from my chair. I did my best to turn my limitations into moments of connection. I'd chase them around baseball diamonds in high gear, or I'd roll back and forth in front of a soccer goal to act as keeper. I'd even let them climb onto my lap as we raced around the house in my chair. That became our version of our normal. Savannah used to get frustrated that I couldn't do some things other dads could do, but later she told me, "Once I realized the chair is what made you extraordinary, I stopped praying for a miracle. I wouldn't trade those *normal* experiences for anything."

Back then, I thought I would quickly find a way to walk again. After all, my little girl was growing up, and I was determined to play the traditional father role at her wedding. I busted my butt to get strong with physical therapy. I convinced myself that hard work would help me walk again. It was naive, but it drove me. In fact, it took me an entire seven years until I accepted the reality that it wasn't a matter of will. I figured that if I was ever going to be able to experience these life moments again, it would be with the help of some serious technology, major healthcare advancements, or a combination of both. I was going to have to think much bigger, much more creatively, and I needed help. Fortunately for me, there were others who were also dreaming big.

* * *

In Denver, Colorado, a group of Arrow Electronics executives had gathered for a simple brainstorming session. The multibillion-dollar tech firm was looking to create its next engineering feat that would change the world. Someone in the room suggested creating a car that a completely paralyzed individual could drive, while someone else in the room immediately thought of this former IndyCar driver who would probably be just crazy enough to say yes. That day in 2013 led to a partnership with Arrow that changed my life.

Throughout these pages, I will get into much more detail, but that initial brainstorm led to a "Semi-Autonomous Mobility" vehicle (the SAM car) that I was able to drive with a tube in my mouth and infrared sensors that detected the movement of my head. What Arrow and I were able to accomplish in a few short years with that car, from racing Mario Andretti around the Indianapolis Motor Speedway to driving the streets of New York City, remains unprecedented. I never thought I'd ever get behind the wheel of a car again, but Arrow made it happen.

Since my crash, I have tried to will my dreams into existence through hard work and determination. Our family motto became *Not if, but when*. Beyond the foundation, the race team, and everything else I work to achieve every day of my life, my ultimate goal has been to walk Savannah down the aisle. I didn't know when that day would come or who the lucky man would be that she'd share her life with or any of the other details. Nevertheless, I told everyone who would listen that walking with her on that occasion was my biggest hope. Then, one day, an Arrow executive, Joe Verrengia, asked the question, *What if we could get you walking again?* Needless to say, it took me about half a second to respond, "Let me think about it . . . *Okay!*" With that, the Arrow team and its innovative CEO, Mike Long, began the lengthy process of developing an exoskeleton that would allow me to walk.

Savannah wondered if the technology would be available whenever the love of her life popped the question. She even admitted later that she felt she had to wait to get married until the exoskeleton was ready. She's always been a stubborn and picky person (no idea where she got that from), so I knew I had some time on my hands. When I first partnered with Arrow, Savannah was only sixteen years old. She hadn't even had a serious boyfriend yet, though later in high school she broke three poor boys' hearts! That's my girl. When each one wanted to ask her out, I insisted I have a chat with them before the first date. We'd sit down at a Sonic, and these nervous boys would tell me about their interest in her. Luckily for me and Arrow, it seemed as if marriage would be a long way off. Savannah was driven, focused on college and her career, and was busy exploring the world. Then she met Adam. From the moment Savannah introduced me to him, I had a feeling he would be the one. I knew my timeline needed to speed up. I called Mike and told him we needed to move quickly on that project of getting me to walk again.

Arrow is the largest global distributor of electronics on Earth. They have access to nearly every piece of innovation out there. And because of that, the company had a relationship with many of the world's top-tier universities, including Vanderbilt University, whose engineering department had created the first commercially viable exoskeleton in the US. In 2020, when Savannah and Adam got engaged, there was no exoskeleton on the market for high-level quadriplegics, but Arrow's and Vanderbilt's engineers began to hone the device. When Joe and Mike told me it was going to be a reality and I was likely going to be able to walk at the wedding, I almost couldn't believe it. Savannah fully embraced the idea. She dismissed any concern about pressure it might put on her special day.

The day my little girl started the next chapter of her life would be the day I would walk again.

For nine months leading up to the wedding, I trained relentlessly to become strong enough to use the exoskeleton. Every session was grueling; it required hours of effort, sweat, and quiet determination. Just a few years earlier, I'd started to face new health challenges, including serious breathing issues that made daily life more difficult. During the months of training and through Savannah's wedding, it was as if the clouds lifted. My lungs opened up. My strength returned. My body cooperated in ways it hadn't in years. I can't explain it logically. It was as if I'd been given a window of grace, just long enough to make the impossible possible. In all the years since, I haven't been strong enough to wear the device again. Looking back, that brief moment in time was a miracle in motion.

The exoskeleton itself was a masterpiece of precision. Every piece had to align perfectly with my hips, knees, and ankles. To make it move, I had to lean my upper body forward, shifting my weight so the machine would respond with a step, and then another. Because I don't have trunk control, someone always had to stand behind me to keep me balanced. That person was Leon West, one of our incredible team members at DRIVEN, the neurological rehab facility our foundation built in Las Vegas. Leon became my anchor. Together we practiced for months—adjusting, strengthening, synchronizing. I even traveled to Nashville several times to meet with the engineers at Vanderbilt, fine-tuning every movement.

Eventually, our training sessions even took us to the streets of downtown Las Vegas, where I was able to walk up and down the block in the exoskeleton. People stopped and stared, cheering us on and filming with their phones, but I wasn't thinking about any of that. All I could feel was gratitude. For my team. For my strength. For the gift of movement. After all the dreaming and all the preparations, I was ready for Savannah's wedding day.

The moment finally came in the spring of 2021, when Savannah and Adam were married. It was the tail end of COVID, and finding a venue near where they lived in California had been its own adventure. But in the end, they chose a beautiful outdoor location near the beach. For years, I'd pictured walking her down the aisle, but the terrain in the one-hundred-year-old grove of trees was so rough that it was all I could do to wheel my chair beside her. Somewhere along the way, I even rolled right over the train of her beautiful white dress—a perfect, unplanned moment that made us both laugh. It was so *us*—the messiness, the humor, the grace. Besides, the moment she walked down the aisle was meant to be about her and her husband. There was something just so beautiful about getting to roll her down the aisle—the perfect celebration of *our normal.*

My dream had evolved from walking Savannah down the aisle to dancing with her. After the ceremony and dinner, the party transitioned to a reception hall for dessert and dancing. I could feel the butterflies in my stomach as the dance approached. It's funny—after all those years of racing at over two hundred miles an hour, risking everything in the name of competition, I'd never felt nerves like this. The Indy 500 had nothing on the idea of holding my daughter in my arms again. This wasn't about pressure or danger. It was about love, pride, and the weight of every moment that had led us here. I snuck away and three people helped me put on the suit. At first, the process took nearly an hour, but with all of the training, we got that time down to ten minutes. I got it on with my fancy clothes, making sure that my pants wouldn't fall down (that would be the bad kind of viral video!).

Few of the 150 guests knew what was about to happen before I walked through the dance hall doors; only my immediate family members had the slightest idea. Leon was positioned behind me to help me look as natural as I could in the device, even managing to stay hidden during the photos. Out of the corner of my eye, I could see Savannah start to lose it when I walked through the door. I don't think she was expecting to feel that emotional. The whole day had been a joyful blur for her, and she wasn't expecting any tears. In the end, she and most of our guests couldn't help it. Her brother and mother were standing next to her when I came into the room and Spencer jokingly nudged her and said, "Get yourself together!" As she finally reached me, she took my hands gently and placed them on her shoulders. When we began dancing, the whole world faded away. It felt like it was just the two of us. In a way, it all felt really normal, almost as if we had been doing it, or dreaming of it, our entire lives. For a moment we were just a father and a daughter, swaying to the music.

The song we danced to was "Daddy Dance with Me" by Krystal Keith. While I was hoping for the best, Savannah didn't quite know what to expect from the moment, and I think that uncertainty made it even better. The moment was ours. Perfectly. When I close my eyes, I can still picture the room. Our guests were smiling, tearing up, and cheering so emphatically behind us. No one knew this was going to happen, but as we danced, everyone saw my dream come true. For the event, we hired a videographer to capture every angle. And when we watch the video today, you can see *everyone* is emotional. There wasn't a dry eye in the house. One of the doctors who had helped save my life after my accident was there that night. She was a mess, crying the whole time! Even though I'd talked about *walking* with my daughter on her wedding day, few people knew we would dance together. No one was sure of it until the moment it happened. And when it did, the room erupted into something that felt bigger than all of us—joy, disbelief, gratitude—all wrapped into one perfect, unforgettable dance.

Training for the moment, I'd had a few near falls, but as we danced at her wedding, everything went perfectly. In all my life, I never measured taller than 5′11″. When I played football in high school, I told people I was 6 feet tall, but that was a lie (sorry, Coach!). Yet, when I was measured in the exoskeleton, I stood 6′1″. I still don't know how that happened; the device didn't add any height to me. I was able to see over the floor of people. I was able to look down at my daughter, and she got to see how tall I actually am. "I love this view," I told her. It was the best view I've ever seen, and I've been on top of mountains, riding in planes around the world, and in the winner's circle at IndyCar events. Nothing has, or ever will, compare to that moment.

After Savannah and I finished dancing, the song changed to "My Girl." Spencer led Sheila out to me. She hadn't been expecting it. I was able to dance with my wife again for the first time in two decades. It felt magical, like being transported back to when we were just two young kids falling in love. The years seemed to disappear. It was a moment we'd both waited a long time for, and somehow it felt both brand new and beautifully familiar. After the dances, I got back in my chair and Savannah and Sheila took turns sitting on my lap as I spun them around the floor.

We knew we could have invited national media to capture the moment, but the day was all about Savannah and Adam, not Arrow and me. Still, the short bit of footage we got was shared on social media and went viral, garnering some fifteen million views. People from all over the globe seemed to be inspired by what we'd done. And we're ready for much more to come in the future, from better technology to medical breakthroughs. One day, with Arrow's help, I hope to leave my wheelchair behind and hang a FOR SALE sign on it.

Some people might have expected a person in my condition to sit the wedding out on the sidelines, to stay out of the spotlight and not go through all the work for fifteen minutes of dancing. That's not me. While dancing with my family was the highlight of my life and the best I've ever felt since my crash in 2000, there is a whole lot more to my story.

2

EXAMPLE TO LIVE BY

MY PARENTS, MARV AND JUDY, met thanks to a bit of good luck. My mother had grown up in Beatrice, Nebraska, with five siblings and a father who was a pipeline worker. Her family knew sacrifice, and she'd grown up with a drive for education and an honest, hard-working life. She was eighteen when she met my father. He was just a year older.

The meeting happened when his friend Kenny agreed to give her and a few of her friends a ride back to college. My mother and her girlfriends didn't have a car, and they were looking at a long bus ride from Beatrice to Lincoln, so Kenny agreed to take them. Well, Kenny, unbeknownst to anyone, had an ulterior motive. After agreeing to be a taxi, Kenny found my father and told him, "Hey, Marv, I've got these three beautiful girls and they need a ride to Lincoln, want to take 'em?" Kenny wanted to stay behind. He was thinking that with my dad out of the way for a few hours, he could try and get some face time with Dad's sister, Cheryl (the two actually got married years later). Little did Kenny know he was matchmaking another couple in the process. Dad, being the chivalrous (or maybe just curious) guy he was, agreed to chauffeur the gals. Mom's best friend sat up front while she and another friend sat in the back, talking away. Even though Mom was in the back seat, Marv couldn't get her out of his head. He fell in love with her big blue eyes. Shortly after that first meeting, my father called her, and they went to a drive-in for their first date.

As a young man, Dad was consumed with cars, so much so that he kept losing his driver's license—not because he misplaced it, but because he kept being pulled over by the cops for speeding. At one point he was thrown in jail for thirty days for driving with a suspended license. His father had no money, especially not enough to get a stupid kid out of jail. So, Dad was forced to stay behind bars for a month. Thankfully, my mom jokes, this was before he'd met her; she would have been so embarrassed! After deciding college wasn't for him, Dad worked a number of odd jobs, from Russell Stover's chocolate factory to pouring concrete for missile sites. He was a farm boy who wore a leather jacket and played drums in a band, but his number one love, outside of Judy of course, was speed.

Racing quickly took over his life. The day my parents got married, my mother had to drive them away from the church because Dad didn't have a license after losing it again for the third time. For what? Street racing of course. In fact, my parents spent their honeymoon at the drag races in Omaha. It was then Mom should have known what was ahead of her! Dad even drove in those drag races without a valid license. That's how *he* wanted to celebrate.

* * *

I was born in Lincoln, Nebraska, on August 15, 1964. My parents lived in a basement apartment that cost about $75 per month. They were happy there, but shortly after my first birthday, we moved to Southern California. We had a little rental home on Jewett Street in Arleta, and Dad had a beat-up motorized go-kart he bought from a garage sale. Once I was old enough, that go-kart became my obsession and, probably, my first real risk. I've joked with my family that I should have been in a wheelchair long before my accident.

When I was a kid, my mother would use clotheslines to dry the laundry, and I remember being about three years old, racing the go-kart around our yard (with no helmet of course) between those laundry poles. Eventually, I ran head-on into one of those big heavy poles with the laundry still hanging on it. I could feel my skull rattle. I saw stars, like in those old cartoons, and I got a huge knot on my forehead that I still have to this day.

A few years later, in yet another feat of genuine genius, I attempted a backflip from a standing position off the tailgate of a pickup truck. It was around the time of the Summer Olympics, and I thought I was Greg Louganis standing on a diving board as I stepped to the edge of the tailgate. When I did my flip, I hit my head (also just like Louganis!) on the truck tailgate and had to be taken to the emergency room. I was crying so hard in the ER that Dad was summoned from the waiting room to quiet me down, but the sight of blood coming down my face freaked him out so much that he had to leave. So much for the big, tough guy!

In 1969, when I was five years old, my Christmas gift was a 50cc Honda and, from that moment, my motocross racing career began. Early on, I raced against actor Steve McQueen's son, Chad, at a local track called Indian Dunes. The track is long gone now, but it was just down the road from where Magic Mountain stands today. Kids often imitate what their parents do, and, in my case, that meant chasing speed. Every weekend, either Dad was racing, or I was. The *nut* didn't fall too far from the tree. My parents still have photos of me at six and seven years old, jumping big dirt ramps nearly ten feet in the air. The moment I climbed on that Honda motorcycle, I knew racing was all I would ever want to do.

Dad worked for a Chevy dealer in Nebraska when I was born, but he let that go and brought us out to California in 1965 to build racecars for a guy named Don Brown. Brown was known as the "Prince of Darkness" for his all-night work ethic, but he was also recognized as one of the top Sprint car builders in the country at that time. Dad thought the job would last about six months, and then we would move back to Lincoln. Well, Don Brown's money ran out even more quickly than anticipated, and my father had to get another job. He ended up as a mechanic for a Chevrolet dealership in North Hollywood.

Dad, who was the oldest of six kids growing up on a six-hundred-acre farm, was driving a tractor by the time he was five years old. A few years later, he began a side hustle taking scrap metal and selling it for extra cash. His father worked the swing shift for the railroad from 4 P.M. to midnight. When his dad wasn't home, young Marv would go around to the neighbors and remove unwanted machinery and equipment. He'd drag it home, disassemble it, and sell the iron. He always said taking things apart was as much a part of his childhood as farming.

When he was thirteen, his father brought home an old motorcycle in a box, and Dad put it together like an expert. Then he taught himself how to ride it. He would drive tractors, cars, and motorcycles on the backcountry gravel roads, often at high speeds. His own dad didn't always appreciate the adventures and would give him a good whooping when he caught him driving where he wasn't supposed to. It didn't matter, though, Dad had discovered his passion. He loved the art of speed more than anything else. He was a quick study academically. He graduated from his small high school in Clatonia, Nebraska, at sixteen. He could do anything he wanted, but he had already decided: Life was all about going faster than the day before.

After he moved our family to Southern California, Dad eventually found himself working as a stunt driver for the movies, including a 1966 picture called *Fireball 500*, which starred Frankie

Avalon, Annette Funicello, and Fabian. That film included a scene at a demolition derby shot at Saugus Speedway in Santa Clarita. It was on that shoot where Dad met a few people who owned a salvage yard. Given his background in scrap metal and engines, my father started peppering them with questions. It was his dream to open his own, but one of the guys told him he'd never make it in the salvage business. That was all the motivation he needed. My dad never met a challenge he didn't take personally. Tell him he can't do something, and he will prove you wrong. He's hardheaded like that. Now you know where I get it from.

Working for Don Brown, Dad met a lot of people, including the guys who owned the building where Don operated out of. They owned another lot in Sun Valley and were set to build on it when they started talking to my father about his dream of owning and operating his own yard. They said if he was serious about it, they'd partner with him. So Dad opened his own business on November 4, 1968. He called it Marv's Chevy Only, because, well, those were the only cars he dismantled. For the next thirty years, if you needed a Chevy part, Marv's was the place to go. Things were so bootstrapped back then. Ever the grinder when it came to his work, Dad had a clever system. He would buy a wrecked car from a tow yard or insurance auction on Friday and pay with a check at closing time to ensure it would not be cashed until Monday. That same day, he'd place ads in the paper for the engine and other valuable parts. On Saturday, he'd dismantle the car, and by Sunday, most of it was sold. Come Monday morning, the original check would clear, covered by the weekend's sales. He'd make a few hundred bucks on the deal and do it all again the next weekend.

At the time, he was still working at the Chevy dealership while getting his new yard off the ground. Just a few weeks after he opened his yard, he was let go from the dealership, effectively for being an honest guy. He was advocating for the customers and trying to build goodwill for the long term. At the time, his boss was more interested in the bottom line. Like many times in my parents' life journey, one door closed and a better one opened.

After he was fired, Dad started to make a few calls to folks who might have some extra work. It turned out his friend Jerry needed some help the very next day on a commercial shoot. Suddenly, Dad was making TV commercials, including one for Smokey Bear. He helped to dismantle cars or build cranes and other rigs, depending on the needs of the director and his expert camera angles. Things were picking up and my midwestern father was making a name for himself in the glitziest town in America.

* * *

While Dad was building his career, Mom got a job through a temp agency working as a bookkeeper for the up-and-coming sporting goods company Adidas. The office was in North Hollywood and a neighbor of ours watched me during the day. I remember she smoked like a chimney, and her husband drove a taxicab. Mom liked California. She went to Disneyland as often as she could; one summer she went over a dozen times. They liked their new home and worked to make a go of it even after the opportunity with Don Brown fizzled. One of the reasons they stayed was because Dad, along with finding good paying jobs, got deeper into the racing culture. He liked racing in Nebraska, but he quickly fell in love with it in Southern California.

Early on, Dad had no time or money for racing, but by 1969, he had found his way in, working what's known as the "chase truck."

It's like a mobile pit crew or traveling service station. It began with desert races like the Baja 500 in Mexico, just south of the border. Dad wondered why in the world anyone would put themselves through that kind of abuse, with all the dirt and rattling around in rough terrain for five hundred miles. A few months in, though, he was hooked, and he'd already built his own truck to compete. The challenge was too great to pass up. Being in the salvage business, Dad learned how to dismantle, rebuild, and breathe life back into totaled cars. So he traded a rebuilt 1970 Cadillac Fleetwood for a Chevy Blazer chassis, and he bartered another car for the engine. Like the Johnny Cash song of that era "One Piece at a Time," he built his off-road beast using the parts from many different vehicles. After a test run at the SNORE 250 in Southern Nevada, Dad was confident the Blazer would survive a desert race, so he took it down to Baja.

Sometimes Mom and I would venture down there with him. It was always a good idea for drivers to look at the courses ahead of time, to make notes on sharp turns and hidden bumps in the road. Since it is impossible to memorize hundreds of miles of desert, making a draft of the course is crucial. They call it "pre-running," and we helped. Mom would be up front in the passenger side, and I'd be in the back seat, sitting in the middle.

One time it didn't go so well for me. From the first bite of those eggs, I knew something about my breakfast just wasn't right. In typical Cornhusker fashion, Dad just said, "Suck it up, it's going to be a long day. You need to eat now because we ain't stopping." I knew something was rotten, but I choked it down because he told me to. Some fifty miles later, as we drove through the desert, that breakfast was all over the back seat and Dad's head. Cleanup on aisle Marv! The irony is that Dad is now a foodie who rates restaurants wherever he goes. From that point on, Dad has always listened to any complaints I had about food.

Today, when people think of professional racing, often IndyCar, Formula 1, or NASCAR come to mind. Those series are just the tip of the iceberg. They represent maybe 1 percent of the racing that goes on in America. The truth is that five days of the week there are hundreds of other races around the country. At each one, there might be two hundred people racing cars on circle tracks, dirt tracks, drag strips, or whatever other tracks they can find or build. That's where the real soul of racing lives and where companies like Bell Helmets and engine builders find most of their customers.

There are weekend warriors, semipros, and every kind of racer in between. Some people will work all week just to spend every last cent they have on their cars for the weekend. Dad maybe wasn't that bad; he made sure the bills were paid and his salvage yard continued to do better and better. Away from work, he was one of those underdogs out there on the weekends chasing speed in the desert against pros like Parnelli Jones and Mickey Thompson. This was the time in off-road racing when I like to say that men were *men*. No air-conditioning, no modern comforts, nothing but grueling, gritty, hands-on dirty work. They ate cans of sardines for meals. It was wild, the racing was dangerous, and it was exactly where Dad felt most alive.

Then, in 1974, when I was ten years old, Dad paid a steep price for it.

3

WHEN TIME STOPPED (PART 1)

IT BEGAN one hot August day in the desert. Dad was leading a race in Mexico when he saw another vehicle coming toward him going the wrong way on the course. In racing, a split second can change everything. Dad tried to swerve, but there was nowhere to go. The vehicle couldn't get out of the way, and that meant real trouble!

In the wake of the accident, there in the desert, Dad's life would never be the same.

The race, called the Ensenada 300, began on August 24, 1974, just days after my tenth birthday, in Santo Tomas, about a hundred miles south of the border. It was a six-lap race around the tiny town that went out to the beach and back up through the rugged hills. Eighty vehicles and ten motorcycles lined up to compete. My father had won the whole thing the year prior. This time, he started the race in pole position, right behind the motorcycles. Each vehicle left the starting line a minute apart. By the second lap, Dad was in front. He'd even passed the faster bikes. That's when he saw it: a chase truck coming back toward the starting line in the *wrong* direction.

The gravel roads were only thirty feet wide and didn't include any side routes leading back to the starting line. The chase truck had just picked up someone who'd crashed and was trying to return the only way possible. It was a dangerous idea, but he decided to go against race traffic. The driver of the chase truck saw Dad barreling toward him and should have been able to pull off, but he didn't. Dad switched sides of the road, but to no avail. There are people who see a pothole or a rock or a stick in the road and for some reason they must hit it. That's just what happened.

At the last second, to avoid a head-on collision, Dad pitched his car sideways. The truck hit Dad's single-seat racecar directly in the side. The impact was brutal, the kind that stops time. Incredibly, Dad was able to get up from the crash. He told people he had a "heck of a headache," but he was still able to walk. He even rode back to the start line in the chase truck that had hit him. His vehicle was badly damaged, and someone else went back for it later. When he returned to the main paddock, Dad seemed mostly okay—shaken, but functional. He took a bunch of Excedrin and drank a few beers and decided to lie down.

Two hours later, he knew things weren't right. Suddenly, he couldn't talk or move. His right side was completely paralyzed. He says he remembers some of the immediate aftermath. A driver found my dad "flopping like a fish" on the ground and called my mother. She was at the race with him, and she quickly called the on-site doctor, Doc Sowers, who took one look at him and said, "You need to get him across the border."

A couple guys got Dad up, laid him in the back of a camper, and drove him the one hundred miles to the US border. Mom said she could tell he was frightened, but he couldn't utter a sound. Despite all this, he only had one visible injury, a small burn on one of his shoulders from the safety net on the racecar. He wasn't bleeding externally and had no bones protruding from his skin, nothing to show how serious his injury really was. When they finally got to the border, Mom told the officer there was a medical emergency and officials rushed Dad to Chula Vista General Hospital, about thirty minutes north. By the grace of God, there was already a neurosurgeon on site. He had been called in to treat a motorcycle rider from the same race who had split his head on a cactus.

The doctor immediately said they needed to do an angiogram, which is a scan that shows how the blood is flowing through the body. At that point, they were still unsure if he had had a stroke, and they were concerned the test could trigger a second stroke for Dad since the dye that was used to see the blood could go up the spine and cause further complications. Mom said that they had to risk it because she knew that is what Dad would choose to do. The angiogram confirmed what they feared: There was swelling around Dad's brain. The doctors said his brain had smacked against his skull so hard that it started bleeding internally and created a blood clot on the left side of his brain, a subdural hematoma. It was causing his vision loss, lack of movement, and inability to speak.

Mom pressed the doctor on what to do next. He hesitated, maybe afraid to make the wrong call, and finally told her they should just let him rest. He added that if Dad lived through the night, Mom should call his parents. Nurses then took Dad to the intensive care unit. He couldn't speak, but when Mom's eyes met Dad's, she could see his fear. Dad, who was just thirty years old at the time, was in and out of consciousness. Today he says he remembers a lot of it, but who really knows.

I wasn't there. I was back in Nebraska visiting my maternal grandparents and cousins. I loved those summer visits every year, helping my grandparents, detasseling corn, going racoon hunting with my grandpa. I'd sit on their big riding mower and drive it around, cutting the grass outside their home, enjoying the simple life. I had no idea any of this was happening with my dad in California. The night after he was admitted, Mom called to tell me Dad had been in a bad accident and was in the hospital. She called other family, too, and a few people came down to California to be with her, including her sister from Seattle and Dad's brother, Galen. He'd been in the movie theater the day of the accident and, just feeling something was off, he strangely got up and left to find out what had happened.

My father laid in his hospital bed for a week, silent and still. He could not speak and could barely move. He could only try scratching out a few illegible things on a piece of paper with his left hand, while his dominant right side remained completely paralyzed. When Mom asked if he wanted a good shower, he perked up. She really wanted to help him communicate, so she bought a set of magnetic letters from a school supply store, the kind kindergarten teachers use to teach the alphabet. Using those, he could finally communicate a few thoughts. One of his first concerns was his racecar. Mom told him some guys had picked it up and not to worry about it. Even lying there, so many unknowns lingering and barely able to move, his car was at the top of his mind.

I was 1,500 miles away and did not understand the gravity of the situation. As time passed, I grew restless. Even though I was only ten, I knew something more was going on than Mom would let on. One night, she called me and I asked her if I could talk to him. He was still noncommunicative, the life seeming to drain little by little from his body like a reverse IV drip. Mom was hesitant, but she held the phone to his ear anyway. I remember it like it was yesterday. I was sitting in my grandparents' back bedroom. When I heard his silence, I knew I had to fly home to see him right away.

By this time, Dad had been moved to UCLA for more testing and to be closer to home and the family business. He'd been taken there in a motor home by Mom and some of his racing friends. When they asked the doctors in Chula Vista if they should use an ambulance, the doctor said that he could have a stroke just as easily in a motor home as he could in an ambulance. So, they went with what they knew. Thanks to a bit of good luck, Dad was able to see the chief neurosurgeon at UCLA, a man named Dr. Eugene Stern. Mom and Dad had been sent there with a manila envelope with his charts and X-rays—not exactly high-tech stuff. However, upon seeing them, Dr. Stern insisted he needed to do another brain scan immediately. When Dad arrived at UCLA, it had been twelve days since the accident, and he still wasn't showing progress. He still couldn't talk or move most of his body. Some of the swelling had gone down in his brain, but Dr. Stern needed new images to see what was going on. When the doctor got the pictures back, he told Mom that he could ask a dozen colleagues how they should proceed and they would be split down the middle, half saying to let him continue to heal and half saying to perform the surgery. "But I can tell you that if this was a member of my family," the doc said, "I'd do the surgery to remove the blood clot." Mom knew their decision: Dr. Stern needed to cut the hematoma out.

Dr. Stern said the operation, if they went through with it, would be dangerous, which is why the doctor in Chula Vista never attempted it. Whether he would be able to walk and talk again was uncertain. After discussing the risks, he left and let Mom and Dad decide. All Mom had was Dad's eyes to communicate with. Still, she knew. She could see in his eyes that he wanted whatever might help. So, she ran right out of the hospital room after Dr. Stern, who was standing at the nurse's station just across the hall. Mom said, "Let's do it." She wasn't positive it was the right move, but she knew it was what Dad wanted.

Dad says now that he knew he wasn't getting better just lying there in the hospital room. Even though he couldn't communicate, he says he knew what was happening and he didn't want to be in the state he was in for the rest of his life. Mom had seen other patients with subdural hematomas during her time at the hospital. She and my father had also heard of others dying because of them, a blood vessel bursting in their brain with no warning. Months later, Mark Donohue, a driver who won the Indy 500 in 1972, died from a subdural hematoma that doctors chose not to operate on. Mom said she'd been told Dad's hematoma wasn't small, either. Some can be the size of a teardrop, but Dad's was the size of a hen's egg.

To this day, talking about it still makes Dad tear up. He knows just how close he was to losing his life. Some said he was never supposed to walk or talk again, but they were wrong. When I finally got to the hospital after flying there with my grandparents, I remember he didn't look good. By then, it was after the surgery. His head had been shaved and there was a big ole zipper on top of his skull. To someone my age, that was very scary. I'd never seen him so fragile, so human.

Six weeks after brain surgery, Dad had made enough progress that the hospital planned to discharge him. On the very morning he was supposed to leave, they spotted something new. He told them his breathing felt like ice picks in his chest, and new scans revealed blood clots in his lungs. They kept Dad for another week to dissolve the clots and get him stabilized. We all experienced so much relief when he was finally allowed to return home. However, going home didn't mean he was in the clear—not by a long shot.

Five days a week for two hours a day, Grandpa drove Dad to Cal State Northridge for grueling outpatient physical therapy sessions. It was marathon work. He still couldn't walk or speak well. Those sessions lasted more than a year and a half. One day when I was off from school, I went to visit him during one of his rehab stints, and

I was traumatized by what I saw from his painful experience. My father looked so weak as he fought to move even a tiny bit, struggling with each of the exercises, barely able to move a hand or a foot. To me, it felt like he was in some kind of prison, not a healthcare facility. Dad yelled and screamed just to simply move his leg a few inches. The aggravation to my young eyes seemed like it was killing him, not making him stronger. Yet I'd never seen such determination and will. It was incredibly difficult to watch my father struggle like that, so much so that I never went back again. I just couldn't bring myself to see him like that.

Now technology has improved to such a degree that what my dad had to go through back then would be unrecognizable. During his rehab, they didn't have the sophisticated equipment we have today. He did mat work, and they worked on the right side of his body with pulleys and weights. As a symbol of his time there, a friend of his got him a T-shirt with a cartoon vulture on it that said, *Patience, my ass! I'm going to kill something!*

Dad never had regrets or blamed anyone for his accident. He got hurt doing something he loved to do. We racers know the risks we take, and he accepted it. What he didn't accept was defeat. The doctors had told him he would never walk or talk again, but he decided to believe otherwise. Through the intense rehab sessions over the course of two long years, Dad eventually started to walk again. He never regained movement in his right arm, so he began wearing a sling for support. His right leg developed some movement, which allowed him to walk with a brace. Despite those limbs not being able to move, he could still feel them—and with that, all the pain. Every motion took grit and determination, but he pushed through it all.

He also got his speech back, slowly and humbly struggling through thoughts until he could complete them. He taught me the meaning of the phrase: *It's not about what happens to you; it's about how you respond to it.* Finally, they kicked him out of rehab saying he was taking a spot from someone else who needed it. So, he went home and continued therapy with self-designed rehabilitation equipment. He has always said necessity is the mother of invention.

* * *

After Dad's accident, I stopped racing motocross. For me, everything was turned upside down. It wasn't that I was scared of the sport. It was more that since he couldn't race anymore, the sport left our lives—and so did my connection with him, for a while. He had been my coach and the driving force behind my racing, but now without him pushing me, I got into "normal kid" sports: basketball, baseball, and football. I basically played the sports my friends did. I was good at most of them. I may have been small, but I was fast. I played point guard in basketball, infield in baseball (where I held the California state record for the most stolen bases in a season), and wide receiver and safety in football. My parents filmed every football game on big ole beta tapes, and I'd use them as training videos to learn how to get better.

Dad had just ordered a new single seat racecar before he went to the Ensenada 300. After he got out of the hospital, we raffled it off to raise funds for his rehabilitation. He settled into his life with his primary focus shifting to his automotive recycling business. As I got into my early teens, I worked odd jobs, ranging from delivering wine out of trucks at the crack of dawn for some of the first Trader Joe's grocery stores to working at an auto parts store. I was a small kid, and I wanted to do anything I could to put on muscle to help me with sports. However, I also knew better than to work at Dad's salvage yard. We were too similar, stubborn and convinced our own way was best. It was the kind of father-son dynamic that would always spark friction fast. Besides, Dad said it was better for me to work for other people, to learn what it meant to take direction and see how different businesses operated. Looking back, he was right.

Since Dad wasn't racing anymore, he began to really improve the business. He was always a forward-thinking guy. Mom likes to say he was wearing leather jackets way before Arthur Fonzarelli, but he saw trends in more than fashion. Dad was one of the first people in the Southern California salvage industry to invest in a progressive computer system to track what he pulled from vehicles. Instead of just having a yard out back where people could scavenge, he knew exactly what his inventory looked like, down to the muffler. This wasn't a free-for-all junkyard, it was a well-documented, clean, and organized automotive recycling facility. Don't ever use the term "junkyard" or "wrecking yard" in front of Dad.

People would call him up trying to figure out how he ran his yard, looking for advice from him. That work ethic served him very well down the road, too, when opportunities came for him to partner with other companies. Dad doesn't have a lot of sayings, but one that he still uses today is, *Work smarter, not harder.* He constantly tried to figure out ways to do things more efficiently. Most insurance salvage auctions, including one he later purchased in South Central LA, operated with handwritten ledgers or had an old guy on site who knew where everything was. Dad always thought, *What if that guy leaves us, what would we do?* So he created a proper inventory system with a little help from a lifelong friend: Willis Johnson, the founder of Copart Auto Auctions.

While Dad's personal racing career was essentially over, his love for it remained. Incredibly, he continued to be involved in the sport for years to come. Dad briefly co-owned a racing team in the late '70s that competed in the Indy 500. He also participated in the Great Race (formerly known as the Great American Race) in the late '80s and early '90s, driving classic cars from New York to Disneyland. All the while, his success in business grew exponentially, seemingly by the day. He would go on to travel the country, opening insurance auto auction locations for Copart and expanding his industrious entrepreneurial influence. In a way, he was setting a blueprint for me. Little did I realize at the time just what his example would mean for me some twenty-six years later. In the meantime, I had to see what college was all about.

4

RIDING THE WAVES

MALIBU, CALIFORNIA. Can't be beat. From the sunny weather to the beaches and the celebrity residents, the coastal town feels like an oasis under a blue sky. It's one of the most beautiful places in the western hemisphere. It's also home to Pepperdine University. Sitting up on the mountains overlooking the Pacific Ocean, it's like a postcard of someplace you'd dream of going.

When people ask me why I chose to go to Pepperdine, I joke and say it was probably the 17:1 student-to-teacher ratio and the high academic rating. The reality is that I chose the school because the campus was beautiful, the beach was nearby, and the girls, well, I heard they weren't bad to look at either. I wanted to get away from home for school, but I didn't want to go too far, so the sixty-minute drive from the San Fernando Valley to Malibu seemed like a good distance. I'd gone on tours at several other schools from Berkeley to the University of California San Diego, but once I stepped on Pepperdine's campus, my mind was made up. It ended up being the only school I applied to—thank God I got in!

In 1982, I graduated from Village Christian High School in Sun Valley at seventeen years old, and I wanted to have a little fun during my last summer before college. After graduation, me and a buddy, Frank Williams, traveled up the coast to the Pacific Northwest to visit my cousin in Seattle. On the way up, we made a pit stop at Lake Shasta in Northern California to see some friends. Ever the daredevil, I thought it would be a great idea to dive off the top of a houseboat docked in the marina. Little did I know that the docks are all tied together with angle iron about 10 feet below the surface. Once underwater, I clipped my head on something but didn't realize how bad it was until I came to the surface and saw the horrified look on my friends' faces. Apparently, there was blood everywhere.

Someone handed me a stack of paper towels, and I went into the bathroom to search my head for the source of the blood. As I combed through my hair, a section of my scalp lifted up . . . Yep, time to go to the hospital for yet another set of stitches on my head. If I ever go bald, I will have quite the road map up there. (Yes, this is example number four of times I probably should have been in a wheelchair long ago.)

When I finally got to Seattle, my aunt called my mom and said, "What the heck, you sent an injured kid up here to see us?" Mom, of course, had no idea about my stop at Lake Shasta, or the trip to the hospital. That was me—Mr. Surprise! I just couldn't help myself. And it was that combination of bravado and restlessness that I brought to school that fall.

When I graduated high school, I was still just 5′8″ and maybe 150 pounds. By the end of my freshman year in college, I had gotten a late growth spurt and shot up to almost six feet. Still, I had a pretty good feeling I wasn't going to go pro at any sport I played. Even if I did have the talent and speed, I didn't want to replace any of my body parts by the time I hit forty (ironic, I know!). So, when I got to college I stopped all competitive sports except the occasional intramural game, and I put my energy toward studying business and entrepreneurship.

Pepperdine was a wonderful place that gave me a great education. Some might find it a tough locale to sit and focus on the books, but I got through with good grades. It was the kind of school where you could go to your professor's house for dinner to go deeper with the subjects. The campus community was friendly and while a larger school might have offered a more diverse set of classes, I knew I wanted to study business, so I was set with the Pepperdine curriculum.

Even back then, I had an entrepreneurial spirit. On the weekends between classes, one of the ways I made money was to throw concerts at a nearby pier or other small venues. I hired bands, set up the site, and sold tickets for ten dollars, and if five hundred people showed up, I could make a solid profit after paying the musicians and overhead. I also bought and sold cars on the side, taking what I learned from my dad and incorporating it into my own life. My drive to make money was less about dollars and cents and more about the thrill of competition and proving what I was capable of.

From a young age, I was aware that I didn't have all the resources other people had. In college, some of my classmates on campus came from rich families, drove Ferraris, and even owned homes in Malibu. That was the kind of wealth there, but I wasn't brought up that way. My dad had a salvage yard. We were a blue-collar family with simple Nebraskan roots and a simple work ethic. From a very young age, I understood that if I wanted something, I had to work to get it or earn it. After seeing my father in the aftermath of his accident and watching him rebuild his life, I knew I had to take control of my life. We weren't rich, but we were resilient, and it would be up to me to forge my future.

Maybe it was because I felt I had to compensate for what I didn't have, but I was often seen as a larger-than-life personality at school. And man, am I glad there was no social media back then! Even before I became a full-time racer, I was strutting around campus in parachute pants, full of confidence and possibly too much energy. I didn't like the fraternity options there at the time, so what did I do? I got together with some friends and we started our own—Lambda Omega Sigma, now known as Psi Upsilon. We were a service organization that did not allow alcohol at our events, but we knew how to have fun. One year, a national TV show came to Pepperdine to film. It was a lip-sync competition. We got six of our brothers and signed up. The song we chose was "Just a Gigolo." We all had mustaches and dressed in Miami Vice pastels. One of our brothers was this heavyset, Jim Belushi–type and so he "sang" lead while the rest of us were his background dancers. We treated it as comic relief, and we won the whole thing. Ever since, the fraternity has hosted its own dance competition to raise money for charity. That's the kind of organization we were at our core: a group that prioritized service, worked hard, and never forgot how to laugh.

When I got to Pepperdine, my parents said they would fund me through college and then I'd be on my own. That's another reason why I chose to study business, so that I could make a decent living once I left school. As an undergrad, I made the decision to stay at Pepperdine to get my MBA directly after I earned my bachelor's degree. They had a new program where you could earn a master's in one year of intensive study. If I took a gap year, I knew I'd never go back. I also knew I would need money to pay for grad school. So, during my senior year of undergrad, I signed up for a TV game show that was shot in LA. You may have heard of it: *Press Your Luck*. It's the one where everyone keeps shouting, "No whammy, big bucks, no whammy!" hoping for their square to land on big money and not that Tasmanian Devil–looking cartoon character, which took all your earnings away.

It was 1986 when I got on the show and as *luck* would have it, I won the episode I was on, as well as the next two, taking home $16,350. Later in life it seemed embarrassing, so I never brought it up. That is, until someone sent me a link from YouTube . . . You can't hide from anything nowadays. On the show, I had the same silly mustache I wore in college to try to make me look older. That same mustache that I shaved off after I turned thirty when I wanted to look younger. The other two contestants on the first episode were Eddie, who was a literal Tarzan impersonator; and Julie, who was a poet and songwriter. For once, I was the most normal person in the room! After finishing my undergrad degree in business administration in 1986, I used my winnings to pay my tuition for grad school. I earned my MBA in international finance from Pepperdine's Graziadio Business School in 1987. Thank goodness, I didn't get a *whammy!*

That little game show may have funded my MBA, but it also reminded me of the thrill of competition. And beneath the degrees and business plans, racing was still in my blood. I didn't know how or when, but I just knew I wasn't done racing. I wasn't going to be an engineer, and I didn't want to be in marketing or public relations for the sport. I wanted to *drive.* And to drive, you have to raise money and find sponsorships. I knew I had to give myself a chance to make it in the sport or I'd never forgive myself. If it didn't work out, fine. But no stone unturned. Yet, after earning my master's, I still did not have the funding to compete. So I went the traditional route and found a white-collar job.

My emphasis in graduate school was in international finance. Pepperdine had a program that sent students to China and Taiwan for a few weeks. I wanted that experience, to travel and speak to alumni who could teach me about the ins and outs of commerce in that region of the world. I knew that in 1999 Hong Kong was going to formally become part of China. I wanted to learn all I could and be prepared for the seismic moment in international business. Pepperdine operated satellite campuses in several different countries, from Asia to Europe, which provided students the chance to fully immerse themselves in foreign cultures. Growing up, I'd been to Mexico and all around the United States with my dad's racing, but I'd never been off the continent until college. While there, I took full advantage of the Pepperdine programs and studied in Germany and England.

Studying abroad changed my perspective of the world as well as what I was personally capable of, but I still didn't feel like I had a clear direction. An opportunity in the healthcare field practically fell in my lap, and I jumped at it because I really needed income. During grad school, I was dating a girl whose father ran a bunch of physical therapy clinics within a larger chain of hospitals. I was working on a healthcare industry case study for school, and he found out his CEO was going to be in town, so he arranged for me to meet with him to help with my research. I drove to a Ritz-Carlton hotel about an hour away from campus for what was supposed to be an hour-long discussion about my project. It turned into a four-hour meeting and dinner with this major healthcare CEO. By the end of it, he offered me a job—one that would normally require a master's degree in healthcare administration. I guess I impressed him with my spirit and initiative because he believed I could learn what I needed on the job.

After graduation, I started the position as an assistant hospital administrator in Downey, California. As is my modus operandi, I dove into the position headfirst. Early on in my tenure with the company, I came up with programs to earn the hospital system more money, or cut expenses, which is what I believed I was hired to do. I quickly got an inside look at the healthcare system, which simply didn't agree with me on several levels.

I evaluated our operations and found major cost-saving opportunities, but the ideas were not well received. It was an important lesson for me to learn. *Oh*, I said to myself, *this is the real world*! At age twenty-three, I started to understand that executives weren't always looking out for the company's best interest. At least, that was my perception. I learned another valuable lesson shortly after that when I had an opportunity to oversee a seventy-bed hospital. I thought I had made it! After accepting the job and transferring to Van Nuys, I was given new orders to turn the hospital into a psychiatric facility, effectively firing 75 percent of the staff. Employees were so mad they slashed my tires and keyed my car. As if those two situations weren't enough, the straw that broke the camel's back came when one of my mentors got into an argument with a doctor. My boss, who was a great, salt-of-the-earth type of person who had devoted his life to the industry, was fired on the spot, seemingly just for disagreeing with the doctor (who happened to control the majority of the census for the hospital). You get the picture.

Those three occurrences really soured my opinion of healthcare and basically made sure I would never work in the industry again. (Yes, it is ironic that healthcare has ended up being a massive part of my adult life.) What I found out more than anything was that the idea of "for-profit healthcare" in many ways is an oxymoron. Too often in these types of facilities, conversations are rarely about patients and quality of care. Instead, they are about the bottom line. I struggled with that mentality, to say the least. In the end, it was a great experience because it taught me that my true desire was to never work for anybody again. And, other than driving for a team owner, I never have.

* * *

While I was working as an administrator, Dad was busy back home expanding his business. A friend of his had started a company in 1982 called Copart that auctioned total loss vehicles for insurance companies. In 1987, Dad sought out a chance to get into the action in Southern California. That also created a new opportunity for me to come in and take over Dad's automotive recycling business in Sun Valley, which I did in 1989. I'd had it with my healthcare job, so I made a deal with him to purchase the business. We knew we couldn't work together, so this would be a win-win. One thing we had always disagreed on was which parts to keep at the recycling facility—he wanted to stock everything, hoping it would eventually sell, and I wanted to focus on the inventory that sold . . . well . . . quickly. So, when I took over, I instituted my system—and we made more money with less inventory, but I never told him that. I respect him too much to say *I told you so.*

Now Dad was working on his new enterprise, County Salvage, and I was twenty-five years old running the operation in Sun Valley.

Three years later, Dad sold his salvage auto auction business to Copart—which went public in 1995. During all of this, my entrepreneurial spirit was just getting started. So, in 1992, I decided to take a leap of my own. I'd expanded my part of the auto business, including adding a dealership to my property, and it was doing pretty well. I took all of the savings I'd accrued from the business, and I decided to invest in a new sunglass company. Everyone thought I was nuts. At the time, I was sleeping in an upstairs apartment at the salvage yard and working my tail off, but things were about to get a lot better.

That year I met an incredibly talented man named Greg Arnette through our family accountant. He had been employee number three with Oakley, but they didn't take care of him like they'd promised. So he left the company and started his own sunglass company, Arnette, out of his garage. Greg, who'd invented the Oakley Blades, knew the design, manufacturing, and marketing sides of the business, but he needed someone like me to help with finances. I never minded taking a risk, especially if I believe in the people I'm working with, so I dove in. *No whammy, no whammy!*

I asked the future best man at my wedding, Jeff Jones, if he wanted in. He declined—a fact I rubbed in his face once the company took off. In just three years, we grew to sell upward of twenty-five million dollars' worth of shades to surfers who didn't want to wear the same sunglasses their grandparents did. I had proved everyone wrong.

I put everything I made between 1987 and 1992 into the company. Despite unfounded lawsuits from fierce competitors, we built Arnette into a powerhouse. Then, Bausch & Lomb, which has a foothold in just about every bit of eyewear, called in 1995. They wanted to buy the company, and we sold it for big money. This was a huge deal for me and created a major opportunity to help finance my racing career and my move to Las Vegas. Racing and starting a family require a big investment, and suddenly I had the money to make them both happen.

I've been lucky in my life. Even from a young age, I've had a knack for understanding how money works. I've always been a multitasker and a risk taker. Ever since I left the healthcare industry, I've been involved in a dozen or more businesses at once. I can be like a dog with a bone: Once I get a taste, I stick to it. Of course, I've made plenty of mistakes along the way. There have been lots of highs and lows. Luckily, the gains outweighed the losses. One of the mistakes I made frequently early on—and I didn't really learn my lesson until later in life—was that I thought I had to do everything by myself. I was a chronic non-delegator. I would stay up until four in the morning, reading every piece of paper, tracking every fax overseas. I was convinced no one could do anything as good as I could. I learned my lesson because that all had to change after my accident.

5

THE ONE

ALL RIGHT, enough about work for a minute—let's talk about my incredible wife, Sheila. We met at Pepperdine when we were both undergrads, and believe it or not, it all started because she went on a date with my roommate. Yep, that's right. The first time I met Sheila she was out with my buddy Andy. I guess I should thank him for that. Obviously that relationship didn't last and meeting her became the best thing that ever happened to me.

Sheila was a year behind me in school, but over time, we became friends. She found out I was a car guy and that my family was all about racing. She told me her dad liked cars too, and he was always fixing up old ones. I thought, *Hey, maybe this could work.* Plus, she drove a Camaro Z28, which—hello, right? To her, a car was just a tool to get from point A to point B. I knew from the start that she was the practical one in the relationship.

Sheila loves to tell the story of how we met. According to her, she "wasn't even looking to date at the time. College was tough—especially at Pepperdine—and Sam? Everything just came easy for him. He's too smart for his own good!" That's how she tells it, anyway. I always laugh when she says that, because for me, it definitely wasn't all that easy. But she wasn't wrong about us hitting it off. We got closer every week. We had a lot in common, and sure, we both thought the other was pretty cute. She told me I was charismatic and funny; I thought she was beautiful, grounded, and very sharp. I could see a future with her right away, but it took a while before we ever actually went on that first date.

Right as we were starting to hang out more frequently, I left for an eight-month study abroad in Europe. And I'll be honest, while I was over there, Sheila was one of those people who never left my mind. It was tough missing her and my parents, but the experience of studying and traveling throughout Europe made it more than bearable. When I got back to Pepperdine, Sheila was one of the first people I saw. She was headed back from class and *bam*—it was like we both froze in place. There was just something about that moment that made me realize things were about to change. After that, we finally started dating in earnest. It was still a little unclear where it was all going, but we knew there was something real between us.

Now, it was my turn to wait. Sheila, wanting to experience all Pepperdine had to offer, decided to study abroad in Germany for the summer. I even encouraged her to go because of the incredible experience I had. I don't think I anticipated just how much I would miss her. So, at the end of her semester, I flew over there under the guise of business and racing. It was definitely more of an excuse than anything else just to stay close to Sheila. I traveled to England and then met her in Germany. Sheila and I traveled for several weeks together through Italy and Greece, and it was in those moments that I realized more than ever how much I couldn't imagine my life without her.

When we got back to Pepperdine, things were getting even more serious. That's when I made one of my biggest mistakes ever—one that still makes me cringe to think about. One night we were in her dorm and I said, "We're at the point in our relationship when I think I should ask you to marry me or we should break up. I'm not ready to get married . . . so I think we should split up." I mean seriously, what was I thinking? Looking back, I cannot believe I was so clueless and shortsighted. Sheila told me I broke her heart that day. Even though we're together now, I still regret it. All she said to me then was, "Okay . . ." What else could she have said? I cannot even imagine the anxiety that I put her through. Looking back, it was a blessing, even if it felt horrible. One of us was way too immature to get married at that time—guess who? Yeah, that would be me.

During grad school, I even found another girlfriend (the one whose dad was involved with hospitals). Somehow, though, Sheila and I stayed friends, which just goes to show how much patience she has. While I completed my MBA, she finished her undergrad degree in sports medicine. We were both moving forward, but in different directions . . . or so we thought.

Despite our post-grad lives, Sheila never truly left my mind. After graduation, she worked as a trainer at a chiropractor's office underneath a big sports club. Looking back, it's ironic that Sheila studied sports medicine. That training ended up being a lifesaver—literally—after my accident when doctors were throwing information at her nonstop about my spine. She had experience working with athletes, stress testing heart rates, and handling soft tissue ailments. When it came to navigating the medical world after my accident, she was way more equipped than I think either of us expected. She had decided that she did not want to be a physical therapist long-term, but little did she know the real challenges that would face us navigating this injury.

Sheila didn't love her job at the chiropractor's office, and she told me she was looking to do something else. At the time, I knew my father needed help with his salvage yard, so that is when I connected the dots. I knew he needed someone reliable and detail-oriented, and Sheila was excellent at everything she put her mind to. So I asked if she'd want to do data entry for my dad's yard, logging parts and inventory, essentially to build the system that ran the business. She needed something to pay the bills and her student loans, so she agreed. Before long, she was indispensable. She learned the ins and outs of the business and how to take stock of each part from engines to headlights. She was diligent and a fast learner. Soon, she was running the entire office and Dad saw her as an integral part of everything he did.

When Sheila started working at the salvage yard, I was trying to work my way up the healthcare ladder at the hospital. When I came back into her life, she was dating someone new. Thankfully, her heart wasn't in it. It wasn't like she was waiting for me, but it was hard not to be hopeful when we reconnected. Life kept bringing us back together in one way or another. Finally, in 1991, after eight years of on-again, off-again romance, we got it right. I was very lucky she didn't hold my boneheaded decision to end things back in school against me still. That time apart was important. I needed to mature and be certain of what I wanted from life. So did she.

Somehow, events kept bringing me back to racing, my other true love. When I left healthcare, I began to compete again. No matter how much the idea of "adult life" pushed me away from the sport, something in my DNA brought me back. On some weekends during high school and college, I would sign up for what's known as *jalopy* racing. Let me tell you, it's not exactly the Indy 500. Instead, you take a hundred-dollar beater and remove the windshield and anything else that might hit you in the head. You install a minimum of safety measures, like makeshift roll cages and seat belts. Then, you take the thing to a dirt track to run around in circles. One of the tracks I'd go to was Ascot Park in Gardena, where guys like Parnelli Jones and Mickey Thompson used to compete back in the day. There would be maybe a hundred guys there with their cars and they'd wet the dirt track down like a pig trough, so it got muddy and slick. Then, you'd race for one hundred laps.

The race was more an act of survival than one focused on speed. In fact, the idea was not to push the gas down as far as it could go, because then you'd just spin your tires in the mud. Horsepower wasn't your friend. If you were good and stayed away from big crashes, which there were lots of, your car could last a couple of seasons. The races never had yellow flags, just green for *go* and red if the track was blocked by a wreck. It was like a scene out of *The Dukes of Hazzard*. It was a lot of redneck fun, but it wasn't exactly serious racing. One of the rules was that every car that competed could be claimed by another driver for five hundred dollars. That disincentivized guys from putting too much money in their jalopies. My vehicle of choice was a 1966 Impala I'd bought for fifty dollars. It had a 327 with a power glide automatic transmission, so it did not have much torque, which was perfect for the sloppy conditions. You'd bring some buddies to help you out and you'd buy them dinner and that was that.

As I started to get more serious about racing, I would frequently get parts from Dad's salvage yard. Every time I went into the yard to get a part or to check on my folks, I conveniently also saw Sheila. That's what led us to dating again. She would even come with me to some of the races, which I loved.

It was around 1991 when I began tagging along with my Uncle Galen, who raced a modified Camaro in SCCA (Sports Car Club of America) events. On the weekends, I'd go out with his team to turn a wrench or take tire pressures. During the week, my uncle owned a transportation and special effects company that built and modified vehicles for commercials and movies. Everyone he worked with loved cars, too. It didn't take long for me to realize that I didn't want to just help out in the pits. So, at the end of 1991, I began looking into how I could compete in sports car racing myself.

While the SCCA isn't the top professional racing organization in the world, it is national and has been instrumental in developing drivers over the years. The SCCA holds races every weekend all around the country and it's a great place to start, especially if you want to go road racing. Their bread and butter is the backyard racer. You don't join it to make big bucks; instead, you participate to learn the sport, get experience, and have fun competing on the track. When I joined, there was one class under the SCCA umbrella that had a ton of cars, Sport Renault. For that class, drivers ran spec four-cylinder Renault engines that you couldn't modify. Spec tires, spec everything. That made the whole thing both economical and, by default, about the driver and not the equipment. If everyone had the same car, it was all about talent. I bought a car for $12,000 from a guy who'd had it for five races, got scared, and quit driving.

The first time Sheila saw me drive was at Willow Springs International Raceway in Rosamond, California, for one of my SCCA races. Although lacking in amenities, Willow has been around since the 1960s and given its proximity to LA, was frequented by Dan Gurney, Carroll Shelby, Ken Miles, and many icons of the sport. Out of more than thirty cars, I was winning my class at Willow Springs almost immediately. Nothing helps a driver's confidence more than a first-place finish. My future in racing looked much brighter after that. Sheila knew my father's history with racing. I don't know if she loved that I risked my neck every weekend, but she did love that I was passionate, excited, and working toward something I cared about. She knew it was dangerous, but when it comes to racing, you can't go into it thinking the worst is going to happen.

* * *

To this day, when Sheila talks about the time I proposed to her, she says she thought marriage was the furthest thing from my mind. She did not have a clue it was coming, even though we had been seeing each other off and on for eight years. She thought the only thing I thought about was racing, but, of course, I was thinking about her, too. She was completely shocked when I proposed to her.

I popped the question in April 1992 when we were on a date in Temecula, California. It was Sheila's birthday weekend, and we'd just had dinner together. We were talking about future plans and dreams. My intention that night was to surprise Sheila with a hot air balloon ride, but we were not able to do that because the weather was too windy. Even though it wasn't the fairy-tale moment I had planned, after I got down on one knee and showed her the ring, she said *yes* and made me the happiest man in the world. We were married on November 14, 1992, on a bluff in Palos Verdes that overlooked the ocean. Truly, we had our whole lives in front of us. Two young kids with all the possibilities in the world ahead—or so it seemed.

6

BETTER TO ASK FOR FORGIVENESS

MY RACING HERO growing up was a guy named Rick Mears. Mears was born in Kansas but grew up in Bakersfield, California. He began his career on motorcycles and driving off-road vehicles like my dad and me. In 1976, he won the historic Pikes Peak International Hill Climb. Then, he was hired by Penske Racing after Roger Penske noticed him in the Super Vee series. He went on to win the Indy 500 *four times* in 1979, 1984, 1988, and 1991. He's also a down-to-earth, genuinely nice guy who comes from a family of racers. He was exactly who I wanted to emulate in my career, both on and off the track: someone who rose up through the ranks and became the consummate winner for a long time.

Racing is exciting and inspiring, but it's also quite expensive. Especially when you're starting out and trying to prove yourself as an unknown. When you've won championships and established your name like Mears, the ultimate goal is to be hired by a great team. And there is none better than Penske Racing. When you're an upstart in your mid-twenties who just got out of a job in healthcare, you have to find other ways to make it happen.

There are literally hundreds of talented drivers racing throughout the country. Unfortunately, their ability to compete at the top level is not always dependent on their on-track talent, but often their ability to find or create the funding needed. To get to where I wanted to be, I was working eighteen-hour days at the salvage yard, living upstairs and working on the racecar in between, driving to SCCA events Friday afternoon, and returning Sunday evening to start the process all over again. I had an E-350 van I purchased at an auction and borrowed my uncle's open trailer. My crew consisted of anyone willing to take notes, clock lap times, and do tire pressures in exchange for crappy food and a weekend at the track.

Like many amateur racers, I was funding my passion through the business, but it enabled me to compete in forty-two races that season, including the SCCA Runoffs at Road Atlanta, on a budget of less than $50,000.

Thanks to Dad's auto auction business and, later, his partnership with Copart, there was money coming into the family that was available to help get my driving career off the ground. I didn't want to abuse the privilege or Dad's generosity, though, and I never let his good fortune mean that I didn't have to work hard. The fact is, he would not have funded the entire program anyway. He believed in hard work and making sure I had skin in the game. Still, if my goal was to be the next Rick Mears, I had a lot of work to do. To come out of Southern California relatively unknown and eventually make the Indy 500, where I could then find *real* sponsors, would take a lot of steps.

Most importantly, I'd have to start winning—and soon. I had to know if I was any good. When it comes to the SCCA, there are two types of races, regional and national. Each earned you points toward the two championships. I wanted to race as much as possible, so I entered both regional and national races held in Southern and Northern California, Oregon, and Washington. I even traveled as far as Texas for a national event with my uncle. Each race usually featured about twenty-five to thirty drivers, so competition was always strong. Friends came with me to serve as my pit crew. We raced Saturdays and Sundays.

It was in 1992 when things really got going for me in all areas of my life. We had changed the operations of the salvage yard considerably since 1989. I'd opened M.A.D. Motorcars, selling rebuildable units, and I'd just invested in Arnette Sunglasses. Oh yes, and then there was the proposal to Sheila, and a wedding date in November. I was at my own crossroads about whether to go corporate or to be a full-time racer. The choice was made for me quickly; I started winning right out of the gate. At first, the drivers in the SCCA looked at me as the upstart at the track (even though I was twenty-seven years old). They would help me with setups and show me some tips here and there. As soon as I started to win, all that friendly stuff changed. They saw me as a competitor. The enemy.

One of the guys who consistently won in the SoCal region was named Lee Fleming. For those who have seen the Pixar movie *Cars*, he's a lot like Doc Hudson. He was about fifteen years older than me, and he had been running in the Sports Renault series for a decade. He owned a motorcycle dealership in Newport Beach, and the SCCA was his weekend passion. It was *his* domain, and I was the young Lightning McQueen. Lee was the type of guy who'd tell you to stay out of his way or face the consequences. In my first SCCA race, I finished third, which raised a lot of eyebrows, including Lee's. People looked at me like, *Where'd this kid come from?* This was my first competition at Willow Springs. I raced every weekend, accruing points and improving my craft. Mix that with working during the week and planning a wedding . . . It was a pretty crazy time.

Not long after my first race at the iconic Willow Springs track, I won, and Sheila was there to see it. That victory convinced me I was not wrong to chase the dream. Fortunately, Sheila and I were such a great match. She was independent and hardworking. She never put pressure on me about my racing schedule or the amount of time I was away from her. It's like that old joke among drivers—their spouses ask, "Why can't we go on vacation?" And the drivers say, "What do you mean, we've been to fifteen places this year." Of course, those fifteen places are all racetracks. Sheila did not make me feel guilty for pursuing my dreams, and she could take tire pressures if I needed her to! She has always been willing to do anything to help my career, and I love her for it.

While the SCCA was competitive, it wasn't necessarily cutthroat—except for Lee. He wouldn't give you an inch on the track. Still, I did well. As I mentioned before, that first year, I competed in forty-two races, both regional and national, while trying to be as frugal as possible. Lee, on the other hand, would do everything he could to take first and beat me, including using new tires for every race. Most people kept the same tires on their cars for two or three events—not Lee. I would watch him and when he discarded his *used* tires, I'd grab them from the stack and slap them on my car, then beat him. There's an extra sense of accomplishment that comes from beating a man with his own tires.

At first, Lee was beating me. By the middle of the season, we were about fifty-fifty. Then, by the end of 1992, I was in the winner's circle all the time. The tables had turned—and fast. Watching that shift happen was pure satisfaction. Nobody else could go toe-to-toe with him. In fact, the guys would start jabbing Lee, saying, "Maybe it's time you hang up your helmet. The young kid's beating you!"

That year, I won Rookie of the Year and ended up beating Lee in the Southern California regional championship, and we both went to the SCCA Runoffs at Road Atlanta. At first, I wasn't even going to go but Uncle Galen was headed there with a team and could transport my car, so I tagged along. There were forty-five cars in that race, the best in that class from all over the country. Both Lee and I qualified in the top six, primarily because we had been pushing each other so hard all season. In the end, I finished third and Lee finished fourth. And he was *pissed*. He wouldn't even talk to me after the race. He was angry not only because he lost the race, but also because he lost to me. I think he would have been happier if he finished twentieth and I was twenty-first, as long as I was behind him. The icing on the cake was that at the season-ending SoCal Region SCCA banquet, I was voted Driver of the Year. Lee didn't attend.

Six months later, I found out Lee and his wife, Linda, lost one of their dogs. They had no kids, a nice house, and a huge yard, a place I would describe as nothing less than dog paradise. Shortly after Sheila and I got married, we got our own golden retriever from a shelter, which we named Ollie after Oliver North. A few months after adopting Ollie, we moved into a duplex house in Long Beach that we bought at a probate auction. It was two blocks from the beach, but it was tiny, maybe nine hundred square feet. Too small for a large dog. We realized eventually that Ollie would be much better off in a home like Lee's. So one day I offered Ollie to Lee. He initially said no, but within twenty-four hours he called back to accept the offer.

There were a lot of tears shed when we gave Ollie away, but it was for the better and it was a nice transition for Lee and me. I was moving up in class, which meant we wouldn't have to race against each other anymore. Years later, Sheila and I would often vacation in Newport Beach to escape the Las Vegas heat, and even after my accident, I'd stop by Lee's shop once a year to say hello. It was full circle from competitors wanting to beat the crap out of each other to friends with respect for one another later in life.

* * *

During my teenage years and my early twenties, my father and I didn't spend a lot of time together. He was growing his salvage business, and I was in school, playing sports and figuring out my path in life. After college, as my journey took me back to racing, it all boomeranged. He started coming to my races, and we had lots to talk about again. Racing was the glue that brought us back together and has kept us connected ever since. Reconnecting with Dad really helped propel me further in my driving career.

I didn't tell my parents about my renewed interest in driving until I bought my first real racecar in 1991. Mostly because, after everything they went through with Dad, I didn't want my mother to worry until I knew I was serious. When I eventually told them, they didn't like it, but my father had always taught me that it's better to ask for forgiveness than for permission. So he couldn't get too mad at me for following his advice. Besides, I was already winning. Up and down the California coast, from San Diego to Sonoma to Seattle, I was setting track records. The idea of ever returning to a suit and tie was becoming less and less of a possibility.

I remember taking my parents to an SCCA event at Willow Springs in 1991 when I was thinking about jumping back into the sport. Uncle Galen was driving in the race, and I wanted to see how my folks would react to the whole thing. One of the best drivers in it was this old fart who was around sixty. Back then, that seemed *old*. Today, not so much! He was a lifer. Well, he started up front in the race, but someone nudged him from behind. He turned backward and slammed against the front stretch wall *hard*, right in front of where we were standing. I gulped. This was perhaps not the best example to show my parents as I considered telling them about my renewed passion. Then the ornery old guy popped right out and was more pissed at the other driver than anything else. Then I thought, *Well, they just saw the worst of it and the guy was fine! Maybe this WOULD work?*

My first huge victory came as an amateur in 1993, the year after Sheila and I were married. After finishing third at the championships in Road Atlanta in 1992, I stayed in SCCA club racing but graduated to the Formula Continental (FC) category, which offered higher speeds and open-wheel cars. Back then, there was a hot young driver named Greg Moore. He was a prodigy who was rising up the ranks and headed to Indy Lights from the USF2000 series. We wanted to make a deal with his father for his car; we knew it was fast. His last race in 1992 was at Willow Springs. He won the championship and as soon as he finished the event, we bought his car, trailer, and all equipment for a tidy $75,000. His engineer, Steve Challis, even stayed on after the race weekend for a couple of days so I could test the car with him and learn from one of the best in the business. Since they were moving on to a new series, they didn't mind giving me all their data and information. After those two days, I ran within three-tenths of Greg's lap times from the weekend before. I was more motivated than ever.

With a new car, everything started to click. All year, I raced in regional and national events, improving with every lap. By the end of the year, I won the national championship in Road Atlanta, a huge milestone that proved I was ready to take on the next challenge. Racing became supremely addictive after that, not that it wasn't already. I joked that it was like crack: just as expensive and just as dangerous. However, it wasn't my only focus. In March, my father sold County Salvage to Copart, Sheila was working full-time for them, and I had joined the company in sales. At the same time, though, I was winning races, and I knew I had to move up the ranks if I wanted to keep my dream of being a professional racecar driver alive.

However, 1994 wound up being more about the family businesses than it was about driving. I felt at a loss—there was no clear strategy for my life in racing. Sheila and I had been married for a year and were living in Long Beach. I was coming off my national championship in Atlanta, but it wasn't like I was being flooded with offers to drive. I managed to run a handful of races in the Shelby Can-Am series, which was a small step up from SCCA. I did it just to keep my reflexes sharp and my foot in the door. At the same time, Copart, which I was working for most of the time, was going public and they needed me to oversee their West Coast expansion from a sales perspective, which included both Southern California and Phoenix. I was practically living on Southwest Airlines.

The next year, though, I found a home. In 1995, racing officials announced the new USAR Hooters Pro Cup Series, which would run twenty open-wheel races on tight oval tracks in Florida, Georgia, and Alabama. I immediately signed up for that. Now thirty years old, I was driving wheel-to-wheel on short oval tracks. Each race paid $10,000 to win. That kind of cash was huge for an F2000 series, especially when our total yearly expenses were about $75,000. The purse brought out some great drivers.

I was finally a professional racer after years as an upstart amateur. Thursday nights after work, I'd take a red-eye flight to wherever the race was, head to the track, then sleep in a rental car for a few hours until the crew showed up. My team was based in Atlanta, and they'd meet me with our car wherever the race was being held. On Fridays, I'd practice on the track for a few hours. On Saturdays, we'd make appearances at a local Hooters—I don't think I'll ever eat another Hooters wing again—and we'd race on Saturday night. Then I would fly back to the West Coast on Sunday morning. The whole thing was a great experience on many levels. Because of the large purse, there were nearly two dozen drivers and crazy crowds each week. I was on a good team and my teammate Anthony Lazzaro, who was a few years older than me, won the championship that season. I earned Rookie of the Year honors. More importantly, the series taught me how to race in close proximity to other drivers without damaging my car. I think I only damaged one front wing the entire season. I won my fair share of races and got a lot of second and third places, too. In the end, I finished third in series points, and I began to really feel that I had a future in the sport. The allure of it just kept sucking me back in.

* * *

The following season, I competed in the SCCA F2000 Pro Series and drove in sixteen races on all types of iconic circuits. I finished third in the national championship and, again, Rookie of the Year honors. I had a lot of top-five finishes in fields of forty or more drivers. I could practically taste the Indy 500, the biggest sporting event in the world. And normally, there would have been a clear path to what was next, but 1996 was the year CART and the Indy Racing League (IRL) split. This was a major event in the sport that would have ripple effects for decades—imagine if the NFL broke up into two football leagues and one kept the Super Bowl, but the other didn't. That wouldn't be good for anyone, especially not for the drivers trying to climb the ladder. Why did it happen? Well, it depends on who you ask. At a high level, it ultimately came down to control, egos, and money. Back then, open-wheel racing was the most popular form of racing in America, but after the split, NASCAR capitalized and took much of the fan base.

That was a tough year to be a driver. Back then, there was a big division in open-wheel racing. If you wanted to stay in the sport, you had to make a choice. With my experience, I wanted to continue road racing, which meant going with CART. On the other hand, I knew I needed to find sponsorship, and the best opportunity for that was to race in the Indy 500, which was part of the IRL, a series that only competed on oval tracks. Also, the IRL focused on American drivers, like me. With every crisis comes an opportunity—because of the split, the sport needed more drivers. It's like the situation in golf today between LIV and PGA or basketball back in the 1970s with the ABA and NBA. Two leagues require more talent. So I took what I saw at the time as the best opportunity and joined the IRL.

7

LIVIN' THE DREAM

BACK IN THE '70S when Dad briefly co-owned a race team that ran in the Indy 500, they used a four-year-old McLaren that they'd bought from actor Paul Newman—*yes, that Paul Newman*. In 1978, his team qualified thirty-second, which was the second to last spot on the starting grid. Only Mario Andretti was starting behind in thirty-third and that was because he had been driving overseas and had someone else qualify his car for him. It was not exactly a glamorous starting position! Still, they made the Indy 500, which is pretty amazing for a hodgepodge group of guys from California. Dad's team entered the car in nine races that year and used something like eleven engines for it. They might as well have been sponsored by duct tape because everything was barely held together. Even then, Dad used to say running that team was like *feeding a constant flame with one-hundred-dollar bills!*

For a small-town Nebraska boy who spent his honeymoon racing at the Omaha drag strip, to be standing on pit lane at Indianapolis was the realization of a dream he could barely have imagined. It was everything he'd ever hoped for—and I got to witness it. My mom and I went to that Indy 500. I was fourteen years old and by then, Dad had been recovering from his accident for about four years. I remember how electric everything felt at Indy. I'd fallen in love with racing at five, sitting on the floor of our California home, watching everything I could, learning about my hero Rick Mears. Now to see it live, it was incredible. Being there in person exceeded every expectation. The size and scope, the number of people, the loud growl of each engine, the planes flying overhead during the National Anthem. The whole thing was a monthlong event with plenty of pomp and circumstance, car shows, meet and greets, and everything else. Walking around, it felt like all the race fans and people involved in the Indy 500 were *my* tribe. I felt at home. From then on, I looked forward to the month of May every year. Once I became a racer in my own right, the Indy 500 was all I could think about. It was my ultimate goal. If I could drive on that track with a chance to win, I would have felt like I had died and gone to heaven.

One thing you learn when you're a driver, or any professional athlete, is that to succeed, you have to be selfish. You must sacrifice so much and give absolute focus to your job to become a winner. Michael Jordan didn't become *Michael Jordan* because he was a kind, generous guy on the basketball court who had a perfect work-life balance. The same goes for racecar drivers who want to win the Indy 500. Everything else in life takes second place to the sport. I understood that and I was lucky Sheila supported me in it. She had her reservations, but more than that, she had my back.

In order to make it to the Indy 500, a driver first has to find a team that needs to fill a seat, as well as bring a bunch of money to the table—we're talking hundreds of thousands of dollars or more. Luckily, I've always been good at marketing myself and creating value for our team partners. In 1997, I was trying to join a team, and I made a boatload of phone calls to team owners. After my previous F2000 series, the obvious next step would have been Indy Lights or Atlantics, but I was capitalizing on the CART-IRL split and I believed I was ready to go straight to the top level. I wanted to trade my 160-horsepower four-cylinder engine and 140 miles per hour speed for a 700-horsepower V8 and 220 miles per hour ride. I knew I wanted to be with the IRL since it had the Indy 500, but most of the established teams like Penske and Andretti were competing in the CART series.

The split opened up great new opportunities for people like me. The key, though, was to bring some of my own funding to the table. I had victories and a national championship, but I knew any team's first question for me would be, "How much cash do you have?" It's a chicken-or-the-egg thing. Once you're running the Indy 500, you can get sponsors—but you need sponsors to get into the Indy 500. The question for me became, "How do I sell myself?" It helped that I had a car already. That was one less expense for my prospective team. I got that car because I was partially self-funded. Rather than spend the funding I had on operating expenses, I purchased a Dallara chassis, which would have substantial value even after the race was over—as long as I didn't crash it. After calling around using an IRL directory of teams, I finally connected with Blueprint Racing out of Rowlett, Texas.

Their team already had one driver, a guy from Albuquerque, New Mexico, named Jim Guthrie. Jim was a nice guy who owned a body shop, so we already had a lot in common. I went down to meet him, and we started the process of working together, like negotiating terms and planning which races we wanted to run. We had high hopes of competing and winning, although to the racing community, we were long shots. He and his team seemed to me to be more like a bunch of weekend warriors. They weren't necessarily big-time professionals with tons of experience. It was more of a by-the-seat-of-your-pants organization, but they were part of the IRL and had a spot in the Indy 500, so I signed on the dotted line. Considering all the options, it was the best deal I could make at the time. I figured if I did well, I could hope to get recognized and move to a better-funded program.

In 1997, I started driving in the Indy Racing League. I didn't enter the season opener at Disney, but I made the second race in Phoenix. In that race I was in sixth place when my right rear wheel came off, and I crashed into the wall. My teammate, Jim, won the race. Our team had a relatively small budget of about $1.2 million for the season—still, I was overjoyed to even be in the mix in my first race. If I did well, I could make about half of our budget back and then sponsors hopefully would help us break even. If anyone is hoping to go into racing to become a billionaire, you may want to find another occupation because it's tough to make money as a driver or team owner. There is a common saying in the sport: *How do you make a small fortune in racing? Start with a big one!*

After the crash in Phoenix, I wanted to make a better showing at the Indy 500, but when we got there, it was a test of our patience. The race was slated for Sunday, May 25, but it ended up being spread over three days because of bad weather. The Indianapolis Motor Speedway is incredible. The track is huge, and you either take to it, or you feel intimidated. While it was a great honor to be at the Speedway, this would be a race to forget. After qualifying twenty-third, I didn't spend much time in my No. 16 car. I was getting some good tutelage from my coach, Gary Bettenhausen, and we were ready to rock—except my car started smoking on one of the parade laps leading up to the start of the race. Since we were on a shoestring budget, we didn't have three or four engines in rotation. We just had two—one at the track and one, unfortunately, back at the engine shop. When my car started smoking, I knew we were done. I was out of the Indy 500 before it even began. It was disappointing. Officially, I came in thirty-first place. *Hey, at least*

I was there. I was one of only three rookies to suit up that day. I'd made it in the door.

After that, my frustration consumed me. I was pissed at the result of the weekend, and I went home Monday. Blueprint's PR rep called me Tuesday evening. She was screaming at me because I didn't stick around for the Indy 500 banquet. I didn't even know I had to. I was just so angry at the results. It was a bad chain of events. When you're not getting the finishes you want, you start second-guessing your team and yourself. I knew I had to find a better situation. We were struggling every which way. So, halfway through the year, after losing another wheel at Texas, I fired the team and packed my stuff and left Blueprint.

In 1997, I made six starts, completed 416 of 1,224 laps, and brought in $224,700 in winnings. It wasn't a great year, but I'd still made the big time, and I was hungry for more. Some considered me a rising star in the sport; I wanted to prove them right.

As great as it was, joining the IRL was not the best part of 1997. Sheila and I welcomed our first child into the world on August 29. Soon we would see just what a smart, sharp, and energetic young woman she would become. Truly, there is no one more like me than Savannah. Her arrival gave everything renewed meaning. I just knew I had to get my career into high gear to achieve my dreams and make my family proud!

In 1998, I signed with Larry Nash's LP Racing team. Nash built an incredible car, and I helped bring sponsorship money to the table. Together, we qualified sixth for the Indy 500 on May 24, 1998, a huge leap from the year prior. I was running up front for most of the race but, if anything, I got overaggressive. I tried to make an inside pass on Davey Hamilton to push ahead for second, but the move failed and I ended up losing control and going backward in turn 3 into the concrete wall. I finished twenty-sixth that year. The speed and consistency were a major improvement from the year before. I was feeling the momentum beginning to build.

Finally, my big break came a few months later when I finished second at the Las Vegas 500K. That's when the racing world really began to take notice of me as a serious driver. That almost didn't happen, though. During the race weekend, I was set to use a freshly rebuilt engine in our car. Somehow, it got lost in shipping and it never made it to the track. The engine in the car was over-mileage and would never complete the race distance. I did the only thing I could do, I started knocking on garage doors to see if anyone had one I could rent.

One person I talked to, Fred Treadway (whose team won the 1997 Indy 500 with driver Arie Luyendyk), said I could borrow one of his. "No problem," he said. I had previously met Fred and his team manager Scott Cronk on the IRL circuit in Phoenix. They were always welcoming, even inviting me into their team's hospitality tent to grab a bite to eat and talk about racing. Maybe they were even feeling me out to see if we had any chemistry as possible teammates. Anyway, as they were rolling the engine out for me, Roush (the company that serviced the engine) said that we could not use it. Apparently, even though Treadway owned the engine, Roush had a stipulation that could keep another competitor from using it. That caused an argument among them and since I didn't want to be a problem, I just walked away. Ironically, the argument would lead me to drive for Treadway in the Indy 500 the following year. Still in need of an engine, I kept beating the pavement, hoping to find something.

Luckily, I found my friend Tom Kelley, who owned a bunch of car dealerships in Florida and Indiana. He said he would loan me the one that had just come out of Scott Sharp's car. It wasn't completely fresh, but he said it would go the distance. We got it, wheeled it over to my car, slammed it in there, and made one final practice session. I was really slow—like, dead-ass slow. Everyone on my race team—the engineer, pit crew, and even Larry Nash—were, like, "What the hell, Sam?" I knew what the issue was, though. The reason I was so slow was that the engine was almost *too* good. The extra horsepower created so much additional speed that the car would not turn when I got to the corner. In racing, we say it has too much *push*. We would all have to put our heads together to come up with a new setup for the race that would allow us to take advantage of the speed.

Previously, I'd been working with an engine built by guys who didn't have a lot to work with. They were a father-and-son team—nice people, but they didn't have the technology that was necessary for the sport at the highest level. They'd done exceptional considering the resources and the parts we could secure, but the new engine had more horsepower than I'd ever driven. We'd been running such a grassroots program that once I got a competitive engine in the car, it was like turning from Bruce Banner into the Hulk, like someone strapped an extra eight cylinders on. I wasn't worried, though. In fact, I was climbing out of my skin with excitement. It was unbelievable and felt like the first real break I'd had in the sport. Now I was ready to go! With my new engine, I started the race in twenty-third and finished *second* (Arie won). I passed people left and right. I said to myself, *Oh, THIS is what racing is like!* With an engine like that we now had a real chance to make some noise.

After the race, to many people's surprise, Arie announced his retirement. Suddenly, his Treadway team and main sponsor, Sprint PCS, needed a new driver. The executives asked around the garages who they should get and it was Arie who said they should sign me outright—you know, the guy who'd just finished second in an underfunded effort with a borrowed engine. The dominos were finally falling in my favor. Before the weekend was over, I also got a call from a vice president at Sprint who said he'd like to have lunch that Monday before he left town. *Let me think about it . . . Okay!*

Immediately after that, though, I called the Treadway Racing team manager, Scott Cronk. I told him straight up that I was nervous for the Sprint meeting. This could be make or break for my future and I asked him what I should do. "Shut up and let him talk!" Cronk said. So, at lunch, I didn't say a word and, well, it worked! Sprint offered me the job, and they said they'd pay for everything. I wouldn't have to turn over every stone to find another dollar in sponsorship money. And with Sprint, I went from a $1.2 million bootstrap budget and a few flashes of brilliance to a $3.5 million *real* budget and a chance at the winner's circle.

The team also had a contract with Firestone tires. They had me drive 4,000 miles around tracks to test their products, which I was totally happy to do. I also had to do about thirty in-store appearances at places like RadioShack and occasional dinners with Sprint higher-ups to shmooze, but that was fine by me, too. This was all part of the deal for making it to the big leagues. And, to top it off, they'd pay me $300,000 salary plus incentives. Scott Cronk asked me if I wanted to let my attorney look at the contract, but I didn't hesitate and just signed it on the spot. If he needed a kidney, he probably would have gotten that too. I agreed to drive with Treadway for the 1999 season.

* * *

In 1998, I'd nearly tripled my earnings from $224,700 to $662,800. Oh, but 1999 would be even better. That year, Arie came out of retirement for one more race, saying he wanted one more shot at the Indy 500 before he said goodbye. Known as "The Flying Dutchman," he is an icon in the sport and someone I truly respected for his prowess on ovals. He'd won the 1997 Indy 500 with Treadway, which that year became the first team to win the pole and finish first and second in the race. The team was known for their saying, *There are two times of year: The Indy 500 and preparing for the Indy 500.* Now Arie and I were teammates for his final 500 and he was incredible to work with. He was an open book with everything he'd learned during his racing career, and I took in every word.

It was a personal highlight to be on that team. Another highlight came in the final practice session for the race on May 27, which is traditionally known as Carburetion Day (even though the cars have not run with carburetors in over fifty years). This is when you are finally able to size up your competition and see what everybody has for race day. That afternoon, I was the fastest driver on the day, clocking 222.458 miles per hour. Unlike every other race, where you only have a few hours between the last practice and the main event, I was able to bask in the glory of being the quickest for a full forty-eight hours before the green flag. In the days prior to the Indy 500, there were multiple sponsor events, press opportunities, and a parade downtown with 300,000 fans, all of them cheering as we were recognized as the fastest car on Friday.

A third highlight came when I started in seventh place and for a dozen unforgettable laps led the Indy 500 . . . before things started to unravel. At the time, Arie was doing great too, as he was leading the early third of the race before his first pit stop. That's when I took over first place. For a few laps, it felt like everything I'd ever dreamed of. Then a yellow flag came out, and I had to pit under the caution. Arie came roaring back and took the lead shortly after. Then from behind, driver Kenny Bräck, the reigning IRL champ, took over the lead. There was a small group of guys that had pulled ahead in the race and Arie, Kenny, and I were among them. I was confident. Then, we came upon a bottleneck of slower cars we'd already lapped. It got pretty tight and I was a bit impatient *again*. In an instant I had to make a choice: I could either take the risk of hitting Arie or try to thread the needle around one of the slower cars. Of course I chose the latter, and I ended up wiping myself out and crashing into the wall in turn 1 on lap 63. Stupid! A lack of patience is something that would haunt me a few more times in 1999. The only consolation is that Arie made the same mistake later in the race and still regrets it as the 500 that got away from him. I feel exactly the same way.

* * *

One race that *didn't* get away, however, came a few months later on September 26, 1999. That's when I WON my first IndyCar race. To make it even sweeter, it was at my hometown track, Las Vegas Motor Speedway.

Ahead of the race, because my last name wasn't Andretti or Unser, I knew I had to drum up some extra attention. I grew my hair long, dyed it black, and grew out my sideburns. Elvis Presley has a special place in everyone's hearts in Las Vegas, so I wanted to look like the iconic rock star. I dressed up and acted like *the King* all week leading up to the start of the race. I even attended sponsor events dressed in gold aviator sunglasses and a red Elvis outfit. *Again*, thank God for no social media.

During the race, I wore a helmet with the Superman logo on the back because a group of fans had nicknamed me "SuperSam." I earned the pole position after a great qualifying run. Then there was a late race scare. I stalled the car on the final pit stop, which put me all the way back to fifth place. My car was so good, I knew if I didn't get back to the front, my crew would kill me. I worked my way back toward the front. I had one last person to pass: Indy 500 winner Kenny Bräck. With only three laps to go, I made the final pass and won the race. My family and friends were all there to see me do it, even my son, Spencer, who was only a few months old.

After that victory, the newspaper headline in Vegas read, "Sam's Town," which was a riff on the name of a casino in the city (you can always trust a newspaper for a good pun). It was great promotion for them. Given all my Elvis antics, I may have looked pretty silly if I didn't get the checkered flag. Thank goodness I didn't have to worry about that. Most IndyCar drivers get their first race win in their twenties; I was thirty-five years old when I got mine. Still, the taste of victory was just as sweet. I remember that day, Bob Jenkins, one of the ABC TV announcers said, "Sam has a huge career ahead of him."

After the win, we partied on the Vegas strip all night, beginning at The Orleans, where it seemed like half the city was waiting for me. I was floating on air the whole time. My Treadway team doused me in champagne. We all deserved that celebration.

I definitely couldn't have won that race without them. It was such a magical moment. We felt like we were on top of the world. Just a few months earlier, we had led a dozen laps in the Indy 500, and now we had just won the Vegas.com 500. The media and racing fans went nuts for the story, too, the conquering hometown hero. It was my crowning moment as a driver. Everything was now truly headed in the right direction, but there's a saying in racing: *You've got to look far enough down the track to see trouble.* And trouble was coming my way.

Everyone knows racing is dangerous. In the 1990s, the cars still lacked many of the safety features they have today. Still, you train yourself not to think the worst, because the moment you start thinking about what negative things could happen, the fear can take over. My family knew that when we got to the level of IndyCar there would be more risks because of the high speeds and intense g-forces. My dream was to drive in the Indy 500 and Sheila worried, but of course she knew I had to chase my goals. Everybody should have that chance. Sheila saw me have bad luck in the lower racing levels and in my early IRL days. From crashes to little things going wrong, she'd stuck by me the whole time. I've always felt deeply grateful for that.

For some drivers it is easier for their family to stay home on race day. I never wanted to be like that. I loved having Sheila and the kids on the road. Savannah logged something like fifty-two flights in the first year of her life. Looking back, it just seemed normal. Having my family around at these high-speed events was the life we chose. While I focused on the task at hand, I always knew they were taken care of. Just as my mother took care of me while my dad was working, I could lean on Sheila for all of that. Our family was growing, and Sheila had a myriad of concerns, from my safety to our kids' future to our finances. She made it crystal clear that we had to be able to send our kids to college. She didn't care about the house or anything like that. She wanted to make sure first and foremost that the kids were provided for. She wanted to make sure we weren't wasting money. Sheila and I were still doing well financially, thanks to the salvage yard and the good fortune with Copart going public. We were making more money than we ever dreamed, but she wanted to make sure I wasn't spending it stupidly. I promised her I'd be smart and that money would never be a problem.

* * *

Through the 1999 race in Vegas, I managed to avoid any serious injury. That changed during the final race of the season. At Texas Motor Speedway that October day, it was bitter cold with drizzling rain—real crappy racing conditions. Like my first Indy 500, the race itself went in fits and starts. We ran ten laps under a yellow flag and then when the caution lifted, there was another crash. When the green flag finally waved, the field bunched together. We went three-wide heading into the turn—me in the middle, another car up high, and Scott Sharp diving low, trying to make a pass. I aimed for the apex, but Scott came up from the bottom, clipped the infield grass, and ran straight into me. There was nowhere for me to go. Wedged between the two cars, I got squeezed out and shot straight into the concrete wall nose-first at about 160 miles per hour. Scott spun through the grass, and somehow, he got back out on the track. I did not.

The crash knocked me out, but only briefly. When I came to, I could tell right away that there was something seriously wrong with my feet and ankles. The safety crew had to cut open the nose of the chassis to untangle my feet from the pedals. That is an experience I never want to relive. I still remember every detail from watching them cut me out of the car to the excruciating pain I felt when Dr. Kevin Scheid reset my ankle in the infield care center. You know it is going to be bad when he says, "It will be better if I straighten this out now," and everyone else ducks to the other side of the curtain before putting my leg under his arm to correct it. It also made for a very long helicopter ride to Parkland Hospital in Dallas.

Once I was stable enough to travel, I was transported to Indiana University Methodist Hospital in Indianapolis, which is home to the best orthopedic doctors when it comes to racing accidents. Scott Cronk, our team manager, was gracious enough to let my family stay at his house. Scott was in charge of watching baby Savannah. She promptly rolled off a bed and landed on her head. After that, we relieved Scott of his childcare duties.

The doctors in Indy reconstructed my feet. I needed four pins inserted in my left foot to hasten the healing, and two toes were partially amputated from my right foot. It was a brutal way to end the year, for sure, after such a high just weeks before, but that's racing.

Despite several near misses during my younger years, this was the first time I actually ended up in a wheelchair. I had steel halos on both feet for several weeks. Sheila hoped and prayed that I would be able to walk again. So did I. The doctor was optimistic; he said there was no reason I shouldn't be back on my feet and driving in about two months. That was all the assurance I needed to reignite my hope. We finished the 1999 Indy Racing League season fifth in points and increased our earnings to $760,900. I had every reason to believe 2000 would be our best year.

8

WHEN TIME STOPPED (PART 2)

WHEN MY CAR SPUN into the concrete barrier of the track in Texas in 1999, it was violent and fast. The commentators and other racers who saw the impact didn't even have to wait for the replay; they knew right away that my legs and feet were in trouble. They were right. The surgeries and the rehab that followed were difficult, but I was determined to get back for the 2000 season. Challenges are what make life exciting, and overcoming them is what makes life meaningful, right? So, my team and I did everything we could to get me back in good shape for, what I hoped, would be my break-out season. I was getting buzz in the preseason. Many people, from media to drivers, even pegged me as a favorite to win the Indy 500 and challenge for the season championship. The Vegas race was often a predictor of who might fare well at Indy because both are held on high-speed oval tracks. Lots of eyes were on our team.

When the new year started, I was beginning to walk again but could not run or train intensely. I wasn't 100 percent, but I knew I could drive. So I traveled to the Walt Disney World Speedway in Orlando, Florida, to run some practice laps and prepare for the first race of the season. I wanted to start the year off right. Fear never crossed my mind. Going into the season, I was hell-bent on winning. I was thirty-five years old and convinced I was in my prime. I wasn't looking back on my success the previous season; I was looking ahead to what I thought would be a year for the history books.

Sheila hated when I got hurt in Texas. That accident landed me in a wheelchair for several months and I had to learn to navigate much of my daily life differently for longer than I wanted. It was almost like foreshadowing. She wanted me to take it easy and let my feet heal properly. She wanted me to be in good shape, both physically and mentally. From her perspective, there was no need to rush. After all, I had truly made it: two great kids, a loving wife, financial stability, and my dream career as a professional racecar driver finally materializing. Deep down, though, I was a racer. I couldn't sit still. I needed to get back in the racecar.

I also wanted to go to Disney to help attract a sponsor. Our deal with Sprint ended after the 1999 season, and we needed a replacement. We had a few leads, but nothing had been finalized. A successful test could help. As a bit of a joke, I slapped duct tape on my baseball cap and scrawled "Your Name Here" with a Sharpie, hoping to catch the attention of potential sponsors. I thought about doing the same on the side of our car, but my team thought better of it.

I raced at the Disney track the year prior and I knew it well, even though it had an odd configuration. The one-mile track was built in more of a triangular shape than an oval, almost like the layout of a baseball diamond. It had three rounded corners and was made to fit in the space Disney could allot for it. Dad went to Orlando with me, and that morning, we were running the fastest laps in practice. For it being only my second day back since the Texas accident that cost me a few toes, we were running *fast*.

Then, everything changed. That afternoon, I hit a bump on the track and lost control of the car. It spun and quickly backed into the concrete retaining wall in turn 2 going roughly 180 miles per hour. I was knocked unconscious. Fortunately, I don't remember anything. Just like it had for my dad, time stopped for me.

Emergency personnel came to my rescue. When they got to me, I'd been unresponsive for about two minutes. The level of care in the world of racing is remarkable. The IRL has a team of medical experts on standby who know, not just the cars, but the drivers, too. They're familiar with every driver's medical history and always have experienced and consistent first responders in attendance when cars are on the racetrack, even on test days. If they had been local EMTs instead of seasoned pros who know how to handle racing injuries and how to safely extract a driver from an IndyCar, I certainly wouldn't be here right now. The IRL's commitment to having a full-time medical team is something I'll always be thankful for. Without the quick thinking and expertise of first responders like Mike Yates and Dan Edwards, I would not have made it off that track alive.

After about five minutes of intense care, they finally got me breathing again. They extracted me from the car and airlifted me, in critical condition, to Orlando Regional Medical Center. Sheila likes to joke that I might have lost a few brain cells during those handful of minutes without oxygen going to my brain, and honestly, she is probably right. There are still gaps in my memory from that day . . . and maybe a few other days since then. Unlike my insanely painful crash in Texas, I have no memory of the Orlando wreck. I don't remember the laps leading up to it, the medics, the flight to the hospital, the first surgeries—none of it. I'm grateful for that.

At the hospital, doctors performed a tracheotomy, inserted gastric tubes, and conducted neurological surgery, including anterior spinal cord fusion between the severed C3 and C5 vertebrae in my neck.

The crash had shattered my spine. I was permanently paralyzed from the neck down.

* * *

When I crashed, Dad knew it wasn't good. Usually when a racer hits the wall and his car comes to a stop, he pops off the steering wheel and gives a thumbs-up to let the safety crew know he is okay.

Not me. I was alone on the track, motionless. Dad happened to be on the phone with my mom when it happened. He was asking her to send a fax somewhere. Then he saw what happened to me and he stopped mid-sentence and managed a fearful, "I just saw Sam crash. I'll call you back." Dad rushed to turn 2. He couldn't see much from the infield grass because the emergency workers were doing what they needed to do to get me out of the car. He didn't need to see. He already knew it was bad. When he saw them get the stretcher out and the helicopter circling to land on the track, his stomach dropped.

At the same time, everyone on the race team was communicating with one another behind the scenes. Ruthie Culbertson, Treadway's lead public relations person, called the team manager with the breaking news. Her voice was trembling. "Sam's had an accident, and it doesn't look good." Scott's first reaction was shock, quickly followed by dread: "Is he going to survive?"

Within minutes they made arrangements to get my wife and kids to Orlando. They also worked with the members of my race team who were with me at Disney. They wanted to make sure everyone was okay as they processed the crash and the unknowns of my condition.

* * *

Two hours after I got to Orlando Regional Medical Center, a doctor came out of my surgery (the first of many surgeries) and told Dad what happened. He said I broke my neck. When my parents tell the story today, tears still come to their eyes. The doctor said I had completely disintegrated my C3 and C4 vertebrae, shooting bone fragments into my spinal cord. The team of neurosurgeons tried to repair the fractured sections of my spine, but it would take time for the doctors to tell the exact severity of the injury and whether my paralysis would be permanent. Regardless, it wasn't a hopeful diagnosis. The doctor compared my injury to Christopher Reeve's, the famous actor, who severely injured himself during an equestrian event and was bound to a ventilator for the rest of his life. This was the same man whose *Superman* logo I wore on the back of my racing helmet. I was conscious but in critical condition. The question wasn't how long it would take to recover, it was whether I'd survive the night.

My wife says she can still remember standing in the kitchen of our Nevada home when the phone rang after the crash. It was my mom calling to tell her I had been in a bad accident. Her knees buckled, and she fell to the floor. Sheila knew I was at the top of my game, but she also knew this was a possibility. We all did. Prior to this, we had hard conversations and filled out legal forms, wills, and trusts. I knew I didn't want to be a vegetable if the worst happened. Still, all that preparation didn't make it any easier for her or anyone else in my family to make the decisions that followed.

Sheila had to move fast. She called her mom, Carol, who flew that same day from California to Las Vegas to stay in our home and watch two-and-a-half-year-old Savannah. It broke Sheila's heart to leave her and Savannah was so sad, not understanding why her mom had to leave her. That night, Sheila, my mom, and six-month-old Spencer, who was still nursing at the time, took a red-eye flight to Orlando. My dad found them a place to stay at the nearby Ronald McDonald House. They slept in a single room with two beds. Sheila was in one bed, and my parents were in the other. Spencer slept in a crib in the closet with the door open. Close quarters, but they were together and that was enough for those early days.

Sheila knew my injury was bad but had no idea just how bad until she arrived at the hospital the next morning. There was no good news waiting for her. My neurosurgeon didn't exactly have the best bedside manner. He told her and my dad that there was little to no hope for me. He said if I lived through the week, they should find me a nursing home where I might survive for a few years. The doctor was convinced that I would never live without a ventilator. That was the first thing he said to her. Thankfully, Sheila and my father weren't going to live with that diagnosis. No chance.

* * *

The first time I remember waking up, I couldn't talk. I had tubes in me everywhere. All I could do was try to communicate with my eyes. They affixed a titanium plate to my spine to stabilize me. Lying there, I couldn't help but think about my dad—how, decades earlier, he'd been in almost the same position after his crash in Mexico. I'd heard the stories my whole life: how he couldn't talk, how Mom used magnetic letters to help him spell words, how they were told he'd never walk or speak again. Now it was me in that bed.

Early on, I didn't have thoughts of suicide, but later, they did creep into my mind more than I'd like to admit. I had to consider questions like: *Do I want to live the rest of my life having to put up with all this, confined to a wheelchair and breathing tube? Do I want to put my family through all this rehab and uncertainty?*

While I was fighting to stay alive and make sense of my new reality, my team was trying to make sense of the crash itself. People from Treadway reviewed videotape from the accident and the computer monitoring systems from the car, but they couldn't fully tell what had happened. There were so many things to figure out. The ironic thing was that I had driven at the Disney oval before and knew it well. I had even won a race there in the F2000 series in 1996, but those racecars didn't go nearly as fast as the IRL car. My engineer later told me that I had been going a half-second faster per lap than expected, which created more downforce. The extra speed forced the racecar closer to the surface, which forced it to get airborne when I hit a bump in the track. That's why I crashed. I was going *too fast*.

Although that is what caused the crash, the biggest factor in my injury was my seat. The back of the seat was, apparently, too stiff, too heavy, and made of too much material. When I hit the wall going backward, my whole body pushed back into it. The headrest, though, was softer. So when I slammed into the wall and my body pushed back into the seat, my head kept going backward while my torso stayed in place. My neck snapped back at the top of the seat and that's what severed my C3 and C4 vertebrae. The impact was so severe that the seat itself even cracked. Since then, car designers have lightened the racecar seat material and made it more energy-absorbing, as well as reduced the rigidity of many of the parts on the back half of the car. Thankfully, many more injuries have been avoided since. You can add "crash test dummy" to my resume, too!

It was, as the saying goes, a perfect storm. I'd crashed at much faster speeds before, including two times at the Indy 500 going more than two hundred miles per hour. Things happen, and most crashes turn out to be minor blips in a driver's career. This crash was different. Rarely do cars back into walls at 90-degree angles; most crashes occur on the sides. It was the angle of the hit and the construction of my seat that led to my injury. I don't blame anyone for what happened.

I put myself in this situation. It wasn't my race team's fault, nor my parents or my wife or kids. I do not even blame God. I put myself in the position to get hurt. And I can live with that—life throws lots of hard things at us; we must power through.

* * *

Before my Orlando accident, Scott Cronk, who'd brought me to Treadway Racing, called me the "complete package" as a racer. He liked that I was educated at Pepperdine and that I understood the business side of the sport. He knew I'd funded my own teams, and he respected my work ethic. I'd once called up every person who owned a suite at the Las Vegas Motor Speedway to see if they wanted to sponsor my car for the IRL race. It was something anyone could have tried to do, but I was the only one who did it. He also liked that I brought some of my own sponsors to the table, including BG Products and others. Scott knew I would make appearances, that I was game for every bit of the job and I'd do everything I could to win.

There's an adage in racing: *How fast do you want to go? Well, how much money you got?* There is often a direct correlation between money and speed, but I seemed to always punch above my weight. Most often, drivers off the track are family-oriented, considerate, and even friendly to each other. We enjoy the camaraderie. However, when the helmet goes on, we will run you over to get even an inch more on the track.

Cronk described my racing style as being "on the aggressive side of sensible." Of course, he was right on the money with that. Racing's fine line is to be aggressive enough to win but not so out of control that you're constantly wrecking million-dollar cars. *In order to finish first, first you must finish.* All the cars are so close in design, all the drivers are so talented that it takes an extra edge to win. Cronk liked me because I didn't have a reputation of being reckless or out of control. The only time I was maybe overly aggressive was in the 1999 Indy 500, but I really thought we had a chance to win that one. Driver error must be avoided. During most races, you spend the first three-fourths of the laps just trying to stay in the fight. Then in the final quarter, you can give it your all for the last sprint for the win.

Now I was facing something entirely new. For the first time, I couldn't rely on determination or skill to pull me through—I had to lean on faith. When I joined Treadway, the team put out these trading cards for all the drivers, and on the back was a question, "What's your secret wish?" Mine was "that everyone would have a relationship with God." I wasn't trying to sound holy or profound; it was just something I believed. Now, lying there with so much of my future uncertain, that belief became real in a way it never had before, and I hoped it never would. There was so much I could no longer control, and I knew the only way I could press on was to learn to hand the rest over to God.

9

SCHMIDT HAPPENS

AFTER SHEILA ARRIVED in Orlando, one of the first calls she made was to my best friend, Jeff Jones. He and I met in grad school at Pepperdine. We were both MBA students, and we clicked. He's about five years older than me, very smart, and a loyal friend. The more mature one of our duo, he always pushed for Sheila and me to get together—to this day, he calls Sheila an angel. Jeff played volleyball at Long Beach State as an undergrad, and we played a lot of intramural sports at Pepperdine together, from flag football to softball. We actually made the championship game in both sports. And in the football title game, I saved Jeff's butt on the last play.

He was linebacker and I was playing free safety, and I remember telling him not to bite on a quarterback fake. That was the only way the other team could win. They had one play to get it into the end zone. If we held them, we'd win. Well, Jeff's man beat him and the quarterback threw the ball downfield. It sailed over Jeff's head as the wide receiver raced down the sideline. Jeff thought he'd lost us the game, but then I came racing across the field and into the end zone. I jumped and picked off the pass and we won.

Something similar happened in the softball title game. In that one, Jeff hit a bomb out past the horizon. Celebrating his achievement, he lollygagged around the bases soaking in the glory of hitting the game's winning run. Out of nowhere, the ball came flying back from the outfield. "Move it, dude!" I yelled. Jeff didn't realize the other team still had a chance to get him out. Mercifully, Jeff crossed home plate just in time. "You gotta be slower than my dad," I joked with him. "And *he's* in a wheelchair!"

In the classroom, Jeff and our friends liked to play pranks on each other. I had a habit of coming to class late *occasionally* and was forced to sit in the front row. But Jeff and the rest of our MBA friends were always in the back of the classroom. They knew I liked to burn the candle at both ends in school and, as a result, I'd sometimes fall asleep during the three-hour lectures. That's when they'd pounce! As my head tilted back and my mouth opened, Jeff and our friends would ball up little pieces of paper and try to toss them into my mouth to wake me up. If one got in, I'd cough-choke myself awake. It was a miracle if the professor didn't notice.

Other times, when I wasn't late to class and could sit with them in the back, we would play our version of bingo. We'd fill out our makeshift cards with terms we guessed the teacher would drone on about. Whoever got five in a row would have to raise their hand and ask the professor a question using the word *bingo* in it—like, "What was the economic bingo theory of 1987?" Then we'd watch the teacher struggle to try and remember if that was an actual historical thing. Oh boy, we were troublemakers!

On yet another occasion, I'd asked Jeff to come with me to one of my early jalopy races in Southern California. Though he knew my family and I were into cars, at first, he didn't know I *raced*.

"Want to come with me down to Ascot Raceway?" I asked.

"Okay, to watch the races?" he asked.

"No, I'm *in* the race," I said. "Have you seen any races before?"

"Well, I guess I've seen a few."

"Okay, because I'm going to need you to be on my pit crew," I said.

"What? I don't know what I could do for you on your pit crew except put you out if you were on fire, Sam!"

"Okay, great, that's exactly what I'd need you to do. It's a circle track and I'm going to drive around it as fast as I can. If I crash,

I'm going to stop and drive out to where you are set up with basic equipment. So, I need you to be there in case I wreck the car or catch on fire, okay?"

"Uhhh," he stammered.

"The only other problem might be if my engine runs out of water. So, if I pull off, I'd just need you to fill my radiator up. There's no hood on the car, so it'll be real quick. If I pull off, it means I got a leak and what I need you to do is pull the radiator cap off, fill it with the water extinguisher and put the cap back on."

"What about the tires?"

"If I have to change the tires, I'll lose the race. The only thing we have time for is to flush the radiator out."

"Okay," he said. "Let's go!"

The funny thing is Jeff never even saw the race that night. He had to wait outside the track, which was where the rudimentary so-called "pit" was. He couldn't see anything from there. So, I guess it wasn't much fun for him. But that's the kind of good friend he is. He was also nice enough not to hold it against me when I called him up at one in the morning to tell him I was going into racing full-time or when I joked with him about how good of an investment sunglasses turned out to be. But now, in Orlando, he was showing his loyalty yet again.

Jeff was home in California when Sheila called to tell him about my accident. I asked him several times throughout the years if he would quit his job and work for my race team but each time he declined, which I understood—can't blame a guy for asking, right? When Jeff hung up with Sheila he called my dad, who was with me in Orlando. Dad told Jeff I was stabilized and that they were working on the next steps. Jeff asked if he needed to go to Orlando, but

Dad told him not to do anything just yet. Dad said he would call when he needed him.

It wasn't long before Dad called Jeff back with the start of a plan. It was clear to Dad that we needed to find a different place to go. The Orlando hospital was good for the immediate aftermath of the accident, but we needed to find a more specialized hospital that would have better options for rehabilitation. My family had received some suggestions, but Dad wanted Jeff to do more research to figure out the next move. Jeff didn't hesitate. He was on it.

Today, Jeff has a company that owns and runs nearly one hundred restaurants. Back then, he had a flexible schedule. He'd just bought a new internet business, but he was his own boss and could put those plans on hold for the time being. That was some good luck. Despite his free schedule, the World Wide Web wasn't nearly as prevalent as it is today. It was hard to navigate and find what we needed. Nevertheless, Jeff and Dad split up the country and started researching and making phone calls. Jeff was home in California and Dad was calling places from a hospital pay phone. They reached out to neurological hospitals, spinal cord rehab facilities, and teaching institutions on my behalf, talking to department heads from Miami to New Jersey to Denver and to Atlanta. Some of the department heads Jeff spoke with seemed indifferent or dismissive—but he didn't give up. He and my family prayed for discernment, for God to open the right door because the possibilities seemed endless. After several long days, they had a list of about ten options. One name kept coming up more than the rest: Barnes-Jewish Hospital in St. Louis, Missouri.

One reason they believed in Barnes-Jewish was because of a man named Pat Rummerfield. His story is remarkable. In 1974 (the same year as my dad's accident), Pat was the passenger in a car that was in a terrible drunk driving accident on the highway. He was twenty-one years old, and it left him paralyzed from the neck down. Miraculously, though, he started to wiggle his big toe one day and he eventually regained the ability to walk. This was back in the day when they allowed a year or even more for inpatient rehabilitation. Pat became the first high-level quadriplegic to regain full mobility in his arms and legs. He's since participated in marathons, Iron Mans, and has even set land speed records in an electric car at nearly 250 miles per hour.

Before he knew the science behind what he was doing, Pat had invented rehab tools and techniques that have since proved to help others with spinal cord injuries immensely. He was just the person I needed to be connected to at that fragile moment. He was an example of what is *possible.* He also happened to follow my racing career and admired me as a driver.

My crash had been well publicized on several sports news shows. Shortly after it happened, Pat heard about my crash from a friend and that it had left me paralyzed. Pat wanted to get in touch with me, so his friend started contacting media members in Florida. They got him the information he needed to find me. Pat started calling my dad several times a day, leaving messages about who he was and what he could do. Dad didn't initially pick up since he didn't recognize Pat's number and was so busy juggling calls, doctors, logistics for our next move. At the same time, Pat, who'd been a consultant to Barnes-Jewish for years, even working with actor Christopher Reeve, contacted the doctors at the hospital on my behalf. When he finally got in contact with Dad, everything began to fall into place. They got the ball rolling for me to transfer to St. Louis.

Due in part to Pat's influence, Barnes-Jewish was on the cutting edge when it came to spinal cord research and treatment. They were working with stem cells in rats and mice and getting real results with their human patients, too. Not only did they boast the most aggressive and hopeful rehabilitation options, but they were also the most communicative and persistent to get me there.

Jeff visited a handful of hospitals on his way to Orlando, but when he arrived in Florida, he met with my family, and everyone agreed that Barnes-Jewish Hospital was the best place. Beyond Pat's strong recommendation and influence, what sealed the deal was the team there: Dr. John McDonald and physiatrist Dr. Cristina Sadowsky, both of whom were leaders in the field of spinal cord injury rehabilitation. They were known for the bold and innovative, sometimes even aggressive, approaches to rehabilitation. They had also collaborated with Reeve. When we found out they were willing to accept me, we were thrilled. Funny thing was that my relative celebrity had nothing to do with it; they simply saw hope for my situation to improve and just wanted to help.

Jeff said there was no doubt in his mind that they would have helped anybody. At Barnes-Jewish, it wasn't about teaching you how to live with your injury. Instead, they had intensive, activity-based training that tried to help improve your way of life. Pat and the doctors there told my family that if they were able to work with me, they would do everything possible to get me off the ventilator and that they'd push me every day to improve. Knowing that I was an athlete and embraced hard work, that was the big selling point. I wanted to be aggressive.

It was decided that I should be medevacked to Barnes-Jewish on a jet, which Dr. McDonald personally arranged. It took the Orlando hospital another week to release me, mostly to ensure I was stable enough to travel. Finally, though, on January 21, I was ready to go.

Our family has a phrase—*Schmidt Happens*—and, well, the night we left Orlando for St. Louis lived up to it in every way. The weather was awful. We hadn't even gotten off the runway and the whole tiny cabin of the plane shook. Seats are removed from these types of aircrafts to allow for the stretcher. Lying on the gurney, my nose was about two inches from the ceiling. Jeff had volunteered to fly with me; they would have had to sedate Sheila to do it. It was so compact that he sat next to my head and a nurse sat at my feet. Other than the pilots, they were the only ones on board. Poor Jeff hadn't been given any medical instructions. The only thing anyone told him was to dampen my lips if the air got too dry.

The runway was bumpy, and the wind was pushing the plane from side to side. Before we even took off, Jeff looked down and saw my breathing tube had popped off! He swears he heard me yelp. "I didn't know how long it had been, but I looked at him and his eyes got as big as silver dollars," Jeff later said. "And so were mine." Jeff looked at the nurse, who remained silent. Panicked, Jeff asked, "What do we do, what do we do?!" She looked at him blankly and said, "What are you talking about?"

Jeff pointed frantically at my breathing tube, convinced I was dying.

"Oh," she said. "Just connect it back together."

"All I could think was, *HOW?!*" Jeff remembers.

"And all she said was, *Just do it!*"

Jeff could see in my eyes that I was trying to calm him down. My eyes had gone from as big as saucers to calm and soft, as if I were trying to speak to him. I was beginning to pass out, and everything was turning white. I was trying to communicate, *Come on, pal. You won't hurt me. Hook me back up!* Amazingly, Jeff figured it out and saved my life. He connected the right tubes, and I was able to breathe again. I started smiling and he gave out a giant sigh that turned into a nervous laugh. Crisis had been averted . . . at least that one.

Before we were able to touch down in St. Louis, the pilots said we were making an unexpected landing. Jeff said, "Wait a minute? *Unexpected?* What are you talking about? Is everything okay?" The pilot told him that the headwinds had been so furious, pushing against the plane so severely, that they'd run low on fuel and needed to get more. We wouldn't make it to St. Louis otherwise. The pilot said, "I *think* we'll be okay." Jeff responded, "You *think?*"

We ended up stopping in Wichita, Kansas, which was way out of the way from St. Louis because they tried to fly around the storm. The flight was fine after that. The pilots got the fuel they needed, and we landed safely in St. Louis—thank God. That was, by far, the most terrifying flight of my life. I'm surprised nobody had a heart attack.

We were supposed to get there by 11 P.M., but by the time we arrived, it was after 2 A.M. Despite the delay, Pat was waiting at the airport for us with an ambulance. I was on my stretcher and groggy from the trip. After landing, we drove to Barnes-Jewish at the Washington University School of Medicine, where Pat and Dr. McDonald had reserved a bed in the ICU. Pat promised that he wouldn't leave my side. He told me he was going to take good care of me. I immediately trusted him. When we got to the hospital, Dr. McDonald and Dr. Sadowsky were there waiting at the ambulance entrance. They told Jeff what was going on and were especially communicative. Dr. McDonald and his staff *cared.* So far, Jeff was the only one from Orlando who'd made it to St. Louis—my mom and dad were on their way and Sheila would arrive soon after going back to Vegas to pack some bags and get Savannah. The Barnes-Jewish doctors made Jeff (and me) feel very secure.

The first thing the doctors told Jeff after I arrived was that they couldn't believe I still had a trach tube. "We have to get that out of him," Dr. McDonald said. "The longer he stays on that, the greater the likelihood that he'll never get off of it." They told us that was one of the big mistakes when it came to Christopher Reeve. His doctors kept him on a breathing tube so long he became dependent on it.

Dr. McDonald had been one of the leading minds when it came to the human heart, but he switched his field after he heard about Christopher and his work with spinal cord research. They wanted to find a cure for paralysis, and they were experiencing breakthroughs until the day Christopher passed away. Dr. McDonald asked me directly what I was willing to do—how far I was willing to go. I told him I was willing to do anything and everything I could to improve my situation. I told him, "I'm a risk-taker and that isn't going to stop now."

After a few days in the ICU, I was transferred to my own room. The doctors continued to conduct various tests because I would fluctuate between having a temperature of 104 and being freezing two hours later. As I learned, people with my injuries create more mucus, and that can be dangerous when you're hooked up to a trach. Pat had to unplug my airway several times in those early days, actually saving my life twice. We would give each other little head butts to say good morning. It was really helpful to have a friend like him, especially considering he had overcome the same injury through hard work and perseverance.

After Orlando, Mom and Dad went to St. Louis to find a place for the family to stay. We didn't know how long it would be, so they wanted to get a nice apartment. Sheila went back to Vegas, packed up the 4Runner, and drove it across the country with the kids. When she arrived in St. Louis, my parents had already found a furnished place for everyone. Looking back on it, I'm glad the kids were too young to really know what was going on. Instead, Sheila was amazing and made them feel as if every new change was just a new adventure. I knew it also helped her to see their little faces during this tough time.

By the time my family had settled in, Drs. McDonald and Sadowsky had outlined a plan. First, I needed to have surgery to stabilize my spine and neck *again*. Then I would have to be weaned slowly off my trach tube. Then there would be long, serious rehabilitation. There was so much to do. As the doctors ran through everything with my family, Jeff remembers lying down on a couch and little Spencer climbing on him to find a good place to nap. Jeff says there was something about Sheila . . . Her confidence and grace worked wonders for helping everyone to maintain hope. And on top of her presence, there was a comforting sense among all of us that we were in this together.

10

THE WILL TO FIGHT

WHEN THE DOCTORS finally removed the tube from my throat, I was able to talk a little bit. You had to listen closely, but one of the first things I said was, "I think I can still make it to the Indy 500." I'd come back from crashes before, so why not now? Sheila laughed softly. I don't know if I even believed it myself, but I knew I had to say it, to try and *will it* into existence. I couldn't let myself lose any determination, no matter how silly it sounded. I knew I was going to try as hard as I could to get as much of my life back, even if I was lying flat on a bed, completely paralyzed.

Much of my willpower came from watching my father rebuild his life after he was paralyzed. We're fighters. I saw my X-rays. I knew the situation and what the doctors were saying, but that didn't matter to me as much as my sense of self-determination. I didn't know what the outcome would be, but I knew I couldn't let go of an ounce of hope. Doctors had told my father he wouldn't walk or talk again after his accident and he's still living a full life today, five decades later, walking and talking. I just had one rule for myself: that I wouldn't do or try anything that could put me back on the ventilator. One thing was for sure, once I was off the ventilator, I never wanted to go back.

Losing my ability to move my body from the neck down was bad enough. Couple that with the possibility that I'd have to live with a ventilator was too much to take. It would require more people to help me, and I would have been hooked to equipment for the rest of my life. I'd never even met anyone who lived on a vent for a long period of time. I was still dealing with cracked ribs, fluid in my lungs, and my body temperature fluctuating between absolutely freezing and desperately hot. I knew I had to get off that machine. I *had* to.

When I got off the ventilator, my first request was simple: to get my hair washed. To make that happen, the nurses put me on a gurney and Pat Rummerfield wheeled me back to a sink and washed my hair. It wasn't exactly a spa, but on the bright side, Pat was very good about not getting any soap in my eyes. It is difficult for others to imagine just how exhilarating the simple act of washing my hair was at the time.

Although I tried to make light of the situation, getting off the ventilator was probably the hardest thing I ever had to do. By the time I'd gotten to Barnes-Jewish, few people outside of Dr. McDonald and Dr. Sadowsky had any hope that I was going to be able to breathe on my own again. The consensus from every other doctor was that I'd be connected to the ventilator for the rest of my life. However, with everything my family had gone through, I had a philosophy: If you don't like the diagnosis, find another one. My new doctors didn't give a flying hoot what others thought was possible. They were blazing their own trails, and I was ready and willing to follow. They started weaning me off the device for five second intervals at first. Then, they just slowly increased the time. Each moment was very scary and felt like I was drowning. My chest would tighten, my throat would burn, and my lungs would scream for air. Soon, seconds turned to minutes, and minutes to hours. Finally, after six miserable weeks, we got the results we wanted. By Valentine's Day 2000, I was breathing on my own. That day, I didn't just start breathing again; I started living again.

Now that I was off the ventilator, I could sleep much better. When you can't sleep, all kinds of things can play tricks on your mind. I started to understand what people meant when they said that sleep deprivation is a form of torture. I was in and out of sedation and feeling the effects of all the drugs the staff had given me. I remember yelling to Sheila, "I'm moving my arms! I'm moving my arms!" But she yelled back, "Then do it again!" But we both realized that I wasn't moving at all. It was just in my head. They call it *phantom* thoughts. I couldn't even move a finger, let alone my arms or anything else.

Well before my crash, Sheila and I had a conversation about *what-ifs*. When we had Savannah, we put together the necessary documents and wills. We knew the risks that came with my job as a racer, and we didn't want anyone left arguing over what to do if the worst ever happened. Sheila had a friend who passed away in a tragic car accident. She saw the pain and chaos that followed when family members were fighting over the kids. We agreed, that would never be us. As part of that conversation, though, we talked about hospital care and the dreaded question, "When do we pull the plug?" Sheila thought she might have to make a decision like that when she had first arrived in Orlando. Thankfully, she didn't, and we all knew the right decision was to *fight*.

If I am totally honest, though, in St. Louis there was one night when my resolve wavered. Sheila and I were alone in my room together at Barnes-Jewish. We were talking about the accident. Sheila asked if I was doing okay. I told her I was all right, but I was also feeling sad and wondering why this had to happen to me. Between my family and my racing career, I was living the dream. Why now? I told her I would work as hard as I could and see where my life ended up. As much as a dreamer as I was, I told her I would be realistic, and I knew this wasn't good. Sheila spoke up and said something I'll never forget. She said, "I hate to tell you this, Sam. But if it had been somebody else, they wouldn't make the impact that I think you're going to make—the *difference* you're going to make because of this."

Somehow, Sheila knew. Somehow, she could see that I would gather the strength I needed to press on. Not only that, but she *inspired* me to be more. No matter what the future held, I saw in her eyes that she trusted me to make the best of it. There was a quiet certainty in her voice, as if she could see past my fear, past the pain, and into a future where we would rise above it all. She looked at me with those steady eyes, and said, "Let's move forward. We're going to do the best we can with what we have and make the most of our time. If this had to happen, there will be something good to come out of it. Marv and Judy raised a wonderful son, and we've built something incredible together. We have a great family. We will be okay." In that moment, if I could have risen out of the bed for just a moment, I would have put my arms around her and thanked her through my flowing tears. She didn't just give me hope—she gave me the will to fight for it.

Later, during a visit to the hospital, a psychologist came in to check on me and asked if I was having any suicidal thoughts. I understood why she needed to ask—it was a part of her job, but it struck a nerve. Humor has always been a way that I cope, so I tried to lighten the mood and joked, "Well, not until you brought it up, and it's not like I could do it myself." She definitely did not find it funny. The truth was, I didn't want to go down that road in any conversation. I knew how fragile my situation was, but I didn't want to give the idea any oxygen. I told Sheila I didn't want to keep talking with the psychologist. It wasn't out of disrespect. I just needed to stay focused on one thing: moving *forward*. I don't want to marginalize this for anyone. Mental health is as important as physical health—sometimes even more so. For some, it can be an even bigger hurdle when faced with new challenges. Personally, I used sarcasm and humor to get me through some of those dark moments, but the reality is I eventually dealt with those thoughts and all the questions of my future thanks to my faith, my wife, and my kids.

* * *

I stayed at Barnes-Jewish for six months. I wouldn't be alive today if it had not been for my doctors there. Dr. McDonald had put me on intensive functional electrical stimulation (FES) training and aquatic therapy. The facility already had a blueprint of exercises and procedures because of Pat Rummerfield and Christopher Reeve. Many doctors were scared to work with Christopher, worried that if he died on their watch, it would not be good for public relations. Not Dr. McDonald though; he was fearless.

I was the beneficiary of all that had come before me. The doctors and therapists I worked with believed that people with spinal cord injuries, as well as those who had undergone strokes or other brain injuries, benefited from physical movement and electrical muscle stimulation. Even though I couldn't move my limbs on my own, if others moved them for me, that would help with circulation and my muscle mass. It was critical to get me upright and on a treadmill to keep my bones strong and prevent atrophy. Every movement mattered. The goal was to restore neurological functions and various connections in my body that could still be activated. I would have worked all day if I had to. I wasn't someone who needed to be prodded to get out of bed. I just needed to know what to do, and I'd do it. I believed I could fix anything through sheer willpower, determination, and perseverance. If it didn't work, so be it. We'd find a different route.

Over the course of my time at Barnes-Jewish, I met other athletes who experienced accidents, including a young woman named Amy who competed in the Olympics. She was paralyzed after an ATV accident. Today, thanks to her work at the hospital, she is a Paralympian. Your attitude can mean so much. That's what Pat preached. He was at my bedside every day. He reminded me, especially on the hard days, that attitude matters. And there were plenty of hard days. There were days with fluid in my lungs, or when my ventilator had to be suctioned just so I could breathe. It was a living hell—but I couldn't give in. Pat wouldn't let me.

And I wasn't alone. My family was my anchor. Sheila, my parents, and the kids were with me every morning for breakfast, and back again every night for dinner. Sometimes Savannah would ask her mom, "Why can't Daddy hug me?" All Sheila could say was that I'd been in an accident. Then Sheila would grab my arms and put them around our daughter. You do what you can to make the kids feel like it's going to be okay. Their love wrapped around me like armor. In the darkest moments, it was their presence, their strength, and their unwavering belief in me that kept me going. Through it all, I learned that resilience isn't about never failing—it's about refusing to give up.

* * *

In St. Louis, I needed a lot of work. My doctors performed an operation called a posterior spinal fusion to prevent further curvature and to strengthen my C2 through C5 vertebrae, which surrounded my damaged ones. There was also a very scary twenty-four-hour period in the first couple of days following the operation when my blood pressure was going through the roof. I could have died at any moment and Dr. Sadowsky was trying to figure out what was wrong. It was extremely stressful for my family, as well as my doctors. While most people's blood pressure is around 140, mine was 250. No one could figure out what was going on. I could have had a stroke, or my mind could have gone into delirium.

Despite all the chaos, I was alert. Dr. Sadowsky remembers that I was lying on the stretcher giving people orders, reminding them which tests I'd already taken. I looked at Dr. Sadowsky and told her she needed to figure out what was going wrong. She probably didn't need me to tell her that! She did a CT scan and realized there was an issue with my catheter and bladder drainage. If they hadn't caught the issue, it could have been over that night. With my injury, I also could no longer control my diaphragm and that drastically affected breathing and speaking. It wasn't easy to manage and has been increasingly difficult over the years, but it is a hell of a lot better than being on the ventilator.

My professional athlete insurance covered my stay at Barnes-Jewish for six months. At the time, that felt like a long road—but in hindsight, it was a gift. Six months of care, rehab, and support gave me a fighting chance to rebuild my life. If that same injury happened to me today, it would be a different story. Most people in my situation now are lucky to get six weeks—six weeks to process the unthinkable, to learn how to live in a body that no longer moves, to adjust to a new reality that touches every part of your life. It's not enough. Not even close.

And it's not just the time—it's the system. The insurance that once offered support is now a battleground that is getting harder to fight year after year. And most people don't have a healthcare background like me. They don't know how to fight for more time and for better care. It's devastating. One moment, your life changes forever and just when you need the most help, you must fight the system that you paid exorbitant premiums into your entire life, the one that is supposed to be there to help you.

* * *

During my stay at the hospital, I saw many patients come and go. While they were there, they weren't getting the time with physical therapy that they absolutely needed. I never took my extended coverage for granted. I worked closely with the staff and doctors to make the most of every day, making sure we used everything my insurance would allow, and then some. I knew what a privilege that was, and it only made me more aware of how unfair the system can be for those who don't have the same support.

Not only that, but we knew Sheila had to learn how to take care of me. Spinal cord injuries return the injured person to an almost infant-like state of dependence. I was so thankful I was able to talk, but I could no longer sit upright. I couldn't control my head, bowels, or bladder. So I had to work to do everything I could to try and restore those functions. One of those practices was on an exercise bike, where my body was connected to wires that sent mild electric currents into my muscles, telling them to move and "ride the bike." Today, technology has advanced even further. Some facilities now have exoskeletons like I wore at Savannah's wedding. They are mechanical suits that help people stand and walk again, engaging their limbs and keeping the body from forgetting how to bear weight. Technology is always advancing, and that gives me so much hope.

As far as my role as a patient, I got high marks from my doctors. I stayed up many late nights in my room with Dr. McDonald and Dr. Sadowsky. We were all curious, out-of-the-box thinkers, and Dr. McDonald and I were night owls. Aside from my care, we talked all about racing, skiing, places we had been to around the world, and even my life at Pepperdine. Dr. Sadowsky later enrolled her son at Pepperdine because of how highly I spoke about the school. We also schemed about how to get more investments for spinal cord research, how to apply for more grants, and how to develop the technologies needed to improve care. We even brainstormed how we could change legislation to give people better opportunities at recovery. We talked about these things well into the night. Sometimes I'd go to sleep at 5 or 6 A.M. just to wake up a few hours later for physical therapy. Keeping my mind engaged—staying creative and inspired—was essential. It kept me going. It kept my hope alive.

Another thing that kept me going was thinking about getting back to the track. Okay, maybe I wouldn't drive in the Indy 500, but I knew I needed to be there again. Memorial Day weekend is when the Indianapolis Motor Speedway comes alive for the Greatest Spectacle in Racing. Even though I'd arrived at Barnes-Jewish in January, I figured I could take a little field trip in May, right? I'd survived a near-death experience, and I'd worked my butt off in recovery—I deserved a little break. So about four months into my time at the hospital, I made plans to escape and head to Indy.

"You're going to need to get permission," Pat warned me.

"Okay, get it then," I challenged him.

True to his talents, Pat was able to get me an "excused absence." Dr. McDonald and Dr. Sadowsky even went with us to the race, though not in an official capacity. So did my nurse, Linda Schultz, who today works as a consultant for the Christopher & Dana Reeve Paralysis Foundation. I'd convinced her to take some paid time off from the hospital. I paid her to be my nurse for the trip. I knew being at the speedway, seeing familiar faces, and feeling the energy of the fans would do me good. Normally, the rule would be that if you left the hospital, and especially if you left the state, you wouldn't be allowed back. If you were well enough to leave and travel, you were well enough to go home. I didn't want to hear any of that. All I wanted to hear were my friends' voices, the smell of methanol, and the revving of racecar engines.

We loaded up a van and drove the 250 miles to Indy. The only problem was our van wasn't built for a quadriplegic in a massive power wheelchair. It was built for a paraplegic (someone who is shorter in their chair and can bend at the waist). Its ceiling was too short. To get in, I had to put the back of my wheelchair all the way down, but I still bumped my head on the ceiling, which made me hit my chair's controls and raise the back of the chair up again! Then, I would bump my head again and hit the controls to go back down. I ended up almost like a ping-pong ball going back and forth! Pat finally decided to turn the whole chair off just for it to stop. It didn't matter, though, because I was so excited to go to my favorite place on Earth. Up until this point, you could count on one hand the number of times I let somebody else drive me anywhere. At the same time, I didn't have much experience riding down the road in a wheelchair. The whole ordeal was chaotic, but, of course, my mind started swirling with ideas about how we could improve vans for people with disabilities.

Once we got to Indy, my Treadway team greeted me with a fundraiser at Sullivan's Steakhouse on the Friday before the race. They wanted to raise money for anything that insurance would not cover. Incredibly, they raised about $400,000. My family and I enjoyed the party, and we stayed overnight in a comfortable hotel with my nurse from St. Louis helping. The next day, we drove back to Barnes-Jewish. We didn't stay for the race itself. I didn't need to see it in person. When we got back to the hospital, people asked where I went. I smiled and said I was across the street getting a hamburger. "I must have fallen asleep," I said. Thankfully, it all worked out.

* * *

Dr. Sadowsky is one of those people everyone instantly admires—smart, compassionate, and full of energy. We developed a deep mutual respect, and she once said something about me that I've never forgotten. She told my wife one day, "Sam taught me that you can be a generous, charismatic human being with just your eyes. He can convey his kindness and genuine interest without saying a word." Then, she added, "Now, when he does open his mouth, he's not taking crap from anybody!" What meant the most, though, was when she said that knowing me changed the way she approaches challenges. Being that she is a rehabilitation doctor, that must be often. "Because of him," she added, "I never say I can't. I ask, 'How can we do this?' And then I work to find a way."

It wasn't always so serious. There was even one time in the hospital that Pat almost killed me! We took a van on a little day trip to see the NHRA drag races when they came to St. Louis. It was hotter than hell and by accident Pat locked me in the vehicle. When he realized his mistake, he looked scared to death. It was just the two of us, and so Pat ran off trying to find security or someone who could pick the lock, or something to smash the window to get me some fresh air before I overheated. Thankfully, Pat found security and they were able to open the van's door. All was well that ended well, but those were a scary few minutes!

It was great to get out, but those moments were few and far between. I was typically on a tight rehab schedule. When you're lying there in your bed paralyzed, you must focus on small, but hopefully achievable goals. You are flat on your back looking down at your feet, just trying to get one of your toes to move a centimeter. It's a very humbling experience. I used to dream about winning the Indy 500, and now I just wanted a toe to wiggle. I spent about two hours a day focusing on it. The big toe is the farthest thing away from your brain. If the signal can travel that far, there's hope for more. If your big toe moves, you can get anything to move. Sadly, mine never moved. There was a little twitch at one point, but nothing more than that. People ask me how I could stay there trying to move a toe, day after day. They asked, "Wouldn't you just rather go home?" And I'd reply, "Yes! I'd rather be racing, too." But I knew I needed to stay, needed to have a routine, work hard, and maintain discipline. If I had gone home and been surrounded by people doting on me or feeling sorry for me, I never would have learned what I needed to do, and my family wouldn't have been trained on how to care for me. You have a limited amount of time to get your life on track there in the hospital and, while it may seem like being surrounded by friends would be best, you really need to work and maximize the time you have. That being said, the friends and family who took the time to visit became a powerful source of strength, fueling my willpower to keep pushing forward every single day. The goal wasn't to dwell on what had happened—it was to work toward getting better. That's what I focused on, five hours a day for six months.

That's what happens when your life changes so dramatically—everything you thought you knew gets turned upside down. It took a long time for me to get used to all the new realities of being paralyzed. When my doctors first put me in a wheelchair in St. Louis, my body couldn't tolerate it. I was incredibly sensitive to any change in position, and even with the ventilator in place, my fever would always spike, or my oxygen levels would plummet. It takes real time, patience, and hard work to adjust, and it can drive some people crazy. I had to retrain the expectations of both my family and me, and honestly, I don't think you ever fully master it. Later on, once I got stronger, the hospital staff reprogrammed my chair to 100 percent power—they knew I could handle a little speed and I needed the excitement. It's funny—before all this, we think we're so busy, so scheduled, so tied to our calendars. Yet, the moment something like this happens, all of that just falls away and you have clarity as to what is important in life.

From a professional standpoint I felt lucky. If I hadn't won a race before I'd been injured, I would have always wondered *what if?* I didn't have to second-guess myself after the Vegas IndyCar victory. I knew I would miss racing tremendously and that it would be hard for a while to even watch the sport on television without being there to interact with the teams and drivers. Somehow, I knew I still wanted to be part of the sport. I couldn't let it go.

I tried to keep a positive attitude throughout my rehabilitation. My schedule had me wake up and eat breakfast around 7 A.M. Then I'd have an hour of free time, during which I'd listen to tapes or watch the news. I'd then get dressed and do two hours of physical therapy before lunch. After a couple hours of rest, I would do another two to three hours of electronic stem on the bike and more physical therapy. Needless to say, I was exhausted by the time dinner came around but always enjoyed sharing that time in the evening with my family. That is what re-energized me to do it all over again the next day! Children have endless amounts of energy. Savannah and Spencer naturally brought so much joy to the room.

I learned every day little by little that spinal cord injuries were more complicated than simply believing in "mind over matter." It would take me many years before I truly felt comfortable in my wheelchair. Beyond the physical adjustments, there were a thousand smaller but significant challenges—how to eat independently, how to get dressed, which clothes are actually functional in a wheelchair, and how to stay active outside of a hospital setting. Adapting my home for optimal independence, building a new sense of community, and maintaining daily exercise routines to maintain muscle mass became essential—not just for recovery, but for dignity. Over time, I realized how fortunate I was to have the support of the racing community and my professional athlete insurance. Many others with spinal cord injuries do not have the same resources. That realization inspired me to do more for people like me, who were fighting the same battles without the support.

When you have an injury like mine, there is no timeline for your recovery—you become a patient for life. The gravity of that reality can be overwhelming not just for you, but for everyone in your life. My family didn't dream of being Indy 500 winners, yet they were left to deal with the repercussions of my crash all the same. It's not only that you can't move your arms and legs, but you also lose basic functions most people take for granted. I don't sweat because my internal temperature controls no longer work. Each day, it takes me hours to get out of bed and get ready. The process can be grueling.

A nurse picks me up and puts me in a chair. Then, they help me bathe, go to the bathroom, brush my teeth, shave, and get dressed. I must do my stretches and exercises every morning. No matter what's ahead, even a 5 A.M. flight or a packed daily schedule, this is my routine. What used to take thirty minutes, now takes hours. To stay alive and tolerate all of this, you have to be motivated and know your *why.*

My *why* was my kids. I needed to stay alive to be their dad, to watch them grow up and to see the individuals they would become. That's what I wanted on a personal level. On a professional level, I knew I wasn't done dreaming. New ambitions were bubbling up inside me, pulling me forward when everything else told me to stop.

11

STARTING OVER

WHEN I CRASHED, my life hung in the balance. For reasons it will take me years to understand—and thanks to the determined efforts of so many people—I survived. One of the people who helped to push me forward was Superman himself—actor Christopher Reeve. After an equestrian accident in 1995, when his horse balked before a jump over a hurdle and threw him forward, his hand got caught in the reins and he landed on his head. The injury left him completely paralyzed, unable even to hold his head up without a special support, and dependent on a team of caregivers twenty-four hours a day. It was a freak accident that changed not only his life, but also the trajectory of spinal cord research forever. Through his courage, fame, and collaboration with Dr. McDonald and Pat Rummerfield, Christopher began redefining what was possible for people with paralysis. If he hadn't been injured before me—and if he hadn't used his platform to advance science and hope—I don't think I'd be alive today. I owe him more than I can ever say, and I've spent so much of my life after my accident trying to follow his lead.

When Christopher got hurt, Dr. McDonald took notice and wondered why there wasn't more being done for spinal cord injuries. When they met, they got to work and made great strides together. Later, when I had the chance to meet Christopher, he challenged me to help him promote awareness of spinal cord injuries, too. I knew I had to try my best for him and *our* population. We even did a couple of speaking engagements together after I got out of Barnes-Jewish Hospital. Sadly, Christopher passed away shortly after—too young—just five years after my crash in Orlando. Decades ago, there was little to no hope for recovery if you had a spinal cord injury like mine. Now, while there is still a long way to go, there are many more options to improve your quality of life. We have Christopher to thank for that.

* * *

In 2000, while I was at Barnes-Jewish, the inpatient rehabilitation area of the hospital was one of the older wings of the facility. There were those ugly "cottage cheese" ceilings and I would stare at them for so long that my eyes would cross. The hospital was building a new state-of-the-art facility down the street, but as that was going on, I was stuck in the basement with the low ceilings. I'd fixate on stains on the ceiling and wonder, *What the heck caused that?* I had so much time during my six months there, and we didn't even have cable television!

It was when I was alone that I lingered on thoughts about what I was going to do the rest of my life. Many nights, I couldn't sleep because I was too cold or too hot or just had too many thoughts going through my head. It was easy to dwell on how much my life had changed and what that meant for my family. It got to the point where all I wanted to do was go home, but in reality, that was just as scary. When you go home, mandatory therapy goes away and it is all up to you to be on top of your regimen. That's why I always encourage patients to demand every last session they can from their insurance, aiming for twice a day if possible.

My time in St. Louis felt like ten years but, at the same time, it also wasn't long enough. Today, patients are lucky to get two months in the hospital to rehab and that's just not enough. The patient's needs aside, it takes more than that amount of time for the family to get trained in how to take care of you, and, if you can afford it, the time to transform your house into a living space that can accommodate you in a wheelchair. It's borderline unethical what insurance companies do to patients today in the name of saving a buck.

I learned more and more about all this as my days wound down at Barnes-Jewish. Because of my background in healthcare, I was able to understand what was happening from both the hospital perspective and the insurance one. I learned that the hospital charges about $6,000 each day for inpatient rehab, and insurance companies don't believe that quad- or paraplegics will be long-term customers, so they work to send them home as soon as possible and deny as many claims as they can. Their priority is not about getting a person healthy and ready to go back to their independent life. It's about the bottom line. The same goes for those with strokes and brain injuries. The message is: *Go home and deal with it yourself.* Entire communities are being written off by insurance companies. I witnessed it firsthand, and I knew I had to do something about it.

* * *

The first time my Treadway team manager Scott Cronk saw me after my accident was when he flew into St. Louis for a visit toward the end of February. I could tell he was worried about my family and me. When I saw him, the first thing I said to him was, "You better not give my seat away for the Indy 500!" I was lying there with a severely damaged spine, still talking about racing. Although I said it with a joking tone, a small part of me said it because I believed I could still do it. Scott was never someone to let an opportunity pass, so he put on the fundraiser for me, rallying the community that had already supported me so much. At the time, it wasn't with any grand plan in mind. He wanted to create something to help my family, to make sure my kids had some money in the bank for college in case my life was cut short after my injuries. Little did he know that gesture would turn out to be the catalyst for the Sam Schmidt Paralysis Foundation, which celebrated its twenty-fifth anniversary while I was writing this book.

The same part of me that didn't want to give up my IndyCar seat was the same drive that pushed me to do more when it came to my health and the health of the others around me. I saw what the fundraiser at the steakhouse did and I knew there was more money out there to help. I didn't need help paying my bills—I had pro athlete insurance and financial stability. But most people with spinal cord injuries don't have either. I knew the healthcare system. I knew that in many foundations, most of the money raised disappears into banquets and overhead. I wanted to build something different, and every day I was becoming more driven to do just that.

My friend Jeff was a major help with creating the original foundation. He was our first chairman and the one who helped me realize that the organization that had been started for me could be steered toward the benefit of others. So, we set up a 501(c)(3) with the aim of helping individuals overcome spinal cord injuries and other debilitating illnesses through research, innovation, and quality of life grants. My forte was getting people into the tent, connecting those in my network to the new effort, from Scott Cronk to partners and sponsors of the race team.

When my six months were up and I prepared to leave St. Louis, I was beginning to understand what my life would look like moving forward. It would take several years before the foundation would grow to what it could become, but I had patience (although that is not a word that is usually associated with me). There's a saying that "God never gives you more than you can handle" and while sometimes I found myself looking to the sky and saying, "That's enough!" I knew that I had found a new purpose, one that I definitely would not have found otherwise. With the Sam Schmidt Paralysis Foundation, I had a fresh start. The great thing about the racing community is that a lot of people want to help when tragedy strikes. We may want to beat one another on race day, but every other day, we're one big family.

At Barnes-Jewish, I would get at least ten to twenty cards a day from fans and motorsports enthusiasts. Nobody else on my floor got anything close to that. No one got the visitors I got either. Once a week, somebody was flying in to see me. In the same way that I had so much personal support, I'd gotten a great deal of financial support from that first fundraiser. It became clear that I needed to shift the focus of my foundation outward. Before my accident, I had no idea how bad it got for other people who didn't have top-notch insurance. It all became clear over time.

When we were preparing to head back home to Las Vegas, we didn't talk much about what life was going to look like. It was easier for us to be in the hospital because we had everyone helping out. To face the future and the unknowns felt difficult. Sheila had to take the kids home before I could arrive. It was hard to see them go. Prior to my arrival back in Vegas, Dad remodeled our house. Fortunately, we had our master bedroom downstairs, and my office was on the same floor. Construction workers changed the flooring, ripping up carpet and putting down tile. We had a hospital bed shipped in for me. We tore out the hot tub in our bathroom to create a bigger shower that I could roll into.

I took a commercial flight home to Vegas. Southwest has long been great for people with disabilities. You board first, pick your seat, and the inflight staff are always willing to help you if you get in trouble. (In hindsight I probably should have taken Southwest from Orlando to St. Louis!) To this day, I fly the airline forty to fifty times a year. This flight leaving St. Louis marked my first time on a commercial plane since my accident in Orlando. At the time I was lucky to have my nurse from Barnes-Jewish fly with me. Sylvia even stayed with us in Vegas for a short time to help my family and me adjust to our new lives. These days, people ask what it's like to walk a mile in my shoes. I can't answer that, I tell them, but I can tell you all about rolling a thousand miles in a chair!

Sheila stopped working when my racing career became full time. Between our travel schedule and raising the kids, she didn't have time for it. Thankfully, she could be a full-time mom. After leaving St. Louis, she drove home and started to get ready for me—if such a thing were possible. Not only did we have to adjust to a new life, but we had small kids—now one year old and three years old—who needed constant attention. At the hospital, there were recreational therapists to play with them, but back in Las Vegas we didn't have a staff of people. We had to figure out a big question: Would Sheila take care of the kids, or would she take care of me? And if it was the former, who would bathe me, who would get me up in the morning, who would attend to my small, but constant needs? In the end, we didn't want the kids raised by a stranger. We joked that if the parenting was to get screwed up, we wanted it to be our fault.

That was one question answered. Next was how could I make that happen and also continue my rehab at home. With my insurance, I was allotted twenty-four-hour, seven-days-a-week care. I negotiated with the insurance company and opted out of evening care in exchange for money to purchase the latest rehab equipment.

Our home became like a gym—treadmill, bike, harnesses, elliptical trainer, and other pieces of equipment that would help my limbs and muscles stay healthy. The kids enjoyed climbing all over it as they got older. Working out daily made me remember my dad and his grueling rehabs. Life sure does have a sense of humor.

To get around, I had the latest head-controlled wheelchair, the Quickie 646. The kids liked climbing on that, too. There was a time when I had multiple wheelchairs around the house and the kids would use them as jungle gyms or drive them into the walls. Thankfully, no one got hurt! When I wasn't in my chair or in bed, I was walking on the treadmill with my wife and a therapist moving my legs. I also kept up on other treatments—anything I read about, I tried so long as it wouldn't hurt my progress. Short of flying to China or India for experimental injections, I was game for it all. It didn't even need to be FDA approved, as far as I was concerned. Despite the fact that I knew I had a life of hard work ahead of me that was necessary to keep me alive, the hardest part was looking down at my kids and knowing I couldn't reach down and pick them up.

At home, we had a sunken living room, which was two steps lower than the rest of the ground floor. The kids and I would play around in the space before my accident. But the way it was designed didn't allow us to put in a ramp. So at night the kids would be full of energy and roughhousing around the living room and I would be on the edge watching them, sitting there in my chair, wishing I could be a part of it. Sheila would look at me and see the sadness in my eyes. She could just tell it broke my heart.

That was one of the hardest things for me. What made it worse was that the kids' bedrooms were upstairs, which meant I could never be there to put them to sleep. Some things I could work to change, while others I had to accept as my new reality and use as motivation. Years later, we built a new home in Vegas that would allow me to go everywhere in the house. By the time we got the new place built, though, the kids were older and I'd already missed out on a lot.

* * *

When I initially got back to Vegas, I was fortunate to have a home that had been converted for accessibility, a van for transportation, and a family support system that was incredible. The next big challenge was finding the right in-home caregiver to help get me up in the morning and put me to bed at night. Finding a CNA (certified nursing assistant) was extremely challenging. The agency literally sent out candidate after candidate with no success. After about two weeks, I'd gone through every person they'd sent over (totaling about a dozen). No one worked out, due largely to personality conflicts or my level of injury. I'm a tough guy to work for (or so some people have said). Plus, it is a very difficult and personal decision given that this person must assist, or in my situation, do everything for me that I used to do myself. Brush my teeth, shave, shower, and go through the ever-pleasant process of going to the bathroom every day.

Right when I thought I had exhausted my options, though, I met Myra. She'd been living in Reno, Nevada, but her mother had recently passed away and the company she was working for doing in-home healthcare transferred her to Las Vegas. The transfer allowed her to help her father, who lived in nearby Henderson and was not self-sufficient. Then one day, Myra got a call saying they had a guy who needed her help. Myra declined. She said she wasn't ready to leave her dad. They pushed the issue and told her: "You don't understand. This guy has gone through every person in our company, and we need you." That must have convinced her because soon after Myra arrived at our house.

As fate would have it, Myra already had my phone number. One of her good friends happened to be a cousin of mine by marriage. When we left St. Louis, my father had cast a pretty large net looking for assistance, which included all of our family and friends. When Myra was leaving Reno, her friend told her about me, and she saved my contact info just in case. We don't understand just how small the world is sometimes. When she arrived at our house, she introduced herself. Myra is perhaps the most no-nonsense person I've ever met. She got right down to it. "How do they get you in bed every night?" she asked. "I don't know," I said. Myra paused, "Okay, well this is how we're going to do it." She then laid out a succinct plan.

Myra was exactly the person I needed. She doesn't put up with anything. She just does her job and everyone else has to deal with it. While we butt heads at times, to this day she remains the perfect combination of OCD, type-A personality, and the determined, knowledgeable person I need. She's become invaluable to me as a friend, a caregiver, assistant, logistics coordinator, property manager . . . Well, you get the point. She likes to make fun of me because I inventoried my socks. What can I say? I'm meticulous! I numbered and lettered them so that I would always wear the same matching pair. Myra thought I was joking. She says there are far more important things we have to deal with. We started working together five nights a week at first. She'd brush my teeth, give me whatever pills I required, do range-of-motion exercises, and put me to bed. She did this while Sheila got the kids ready for sleep.

I was finally in a good routine with Myra, but Sheila needed help in the mornings. The agency was on a mission to find another CNA to give her some relief. High-level quadriplegics only make up about 5 percent of the spinal cord injured population. Usually, you have at least hand or arm movement that can assist with some parts of the process. Because of my situation, they could not find anyone with this kind of experience or expertise. We literally had people show up, take one look at me, and ask, "How do you get out of bed?" Needless to say, that was yet another morning that Sheila had to get me up. We found ourselves lowering our expectations just to give Sheila a break, or when we found someone that was mostly acceptable, they would leave after thirty days for a better paying job in a hospital. The situation is one of the primary barriers to people getting back into life after a disabling injury, and it has only gotten worse over time.

Finally, in June 2001, eleven months after my return from the hospital, in walked Anna Bravo, her name at the time. I'm sure that my face and eyes did not communicate a sense of confidence. She was all of 5′4″ and "somewhat" chubby (her words, not mine). She had a few tattoos with story after story to go with them. By this time, I was really trying hard not to judge a book by its cover. She was perky, starting off with "Hello. my name is Anna. I'm going to be your CNA today." If you would've told me that morning, that this would be the beginning of a twenty-five-year-and-counting relationship, I would have said you're out of your mind. Sitting here today, I can honestly say we would not have been able to accomplish what we have without her being in our lives.

I finally had help from the moment I woke up until the moment I went to sleep. Anna took the morning shift when I was home in

Vegas, and Myra basically handled everything else, including traveling with me. Those two do everything from making sure I do my exercises to emptying my pee bag. The reality of living with round-the-clock care can be overwhelming or downright absurd, and I've learned to lean into the humor whenever possible. Eventually Myra questioned why there was no one there for me on weekend nights. She knew Sheila was putting me to bed on those nights, and she felt Sheila had enough going on already, especially with two young kids in the house. Myra had a solution. She decided to work seven nights a week. That's Myra. She makes things happen, and she never takes no for an answer when a situation doesn't feel right.

Two years after my accident, my insurance ran out. We had to find another way to operate. First, I asked Anna if she would do the morning program as a private contractor whenever I was in town. Thank God she agreed. Between getting out of bed, the forty minutes of exercises, bathing, shaving, brushing my teeth, and getting dressed, the whole process takes about two and a half hours.

Second, I asked Myra if she would consider being full-time (more than full-time more often than not). She told me a number, and we agreed. So she started coming in the morning and doing the range-of-motion exercises and then physical therapy. If I didn't do all that work, it would be as if the entire time at Barnes-Jewish had been a waste of effort. It's laborious, to be sure. It's only worth doing if I had a bigger purpose in mind, which I was still developing.

In the meantime, Sheila was baffled that Myra and I got along. We'd be at each other's throats and Sheila would wonder how it was a healthy relationship. Despite some of those heated debates, everyone could see that she was helping me. Myra filled a role no one else could. We're both detail-oriented, direct, and stubborn as hell.

Myra likes to say we're "functionally dysfunctional." She thinks people coddle me, so she makes up for it by holding me accountable. I hate to admit it, but she's right. People don't always treat people in my condition like they would able-bodied folks. They tiptoe. They go soft. They hesitate to push back. But Myra is the opposite. When I'm being a dumbass, she tells me to quit it and slaps me on the forehead (because she knows that's where I can feel it). She'll say, "I don't care if you sit on your butt all day, you don't get to do that!" She thinks people walk on eggshells around me, but she calls it out when she sees it. "Sam wasn't walking across the street when he got hit. He was living his dream. I can't feel sorry for him." That's Myra. She definitely thinks keeping me grounded is part of her job description!

Over the years, Myra only threatened to quit once. Technically, she did. As we worked more and more together, she began to take on more responsibilities. She wasn't just my in-home caregiver in Vegas. She traveled with me, acted as my assistant, and basically knew everything that I was working on professionally. It felt like she was with me all day, every day—including helping me run my foundation. In the early days, we were running things on a shoestring budget. Myra and I put on the fundraiser every year and our board and staff were entirely volunteer. Around 2016, we hired someone who had worked with Christopher Reeve's foundation to be our new CEO. She was our first full-time paid employee. Unfortunately, Myra and the new CEO did not get along. Myra can be abrupt or curt with people that she disagrees with. She is focused and driven, and it's been a huge help for me, but she can also rub people the wrong way at times. She felt like she was doing too much of the new person's job. It got so bad that she said one day, "I can't do this anymore. It's either *her* or *me*." I didn't act fast enough for Myra's liking and so she quit one afternoon when we were at a racing event. Shortly after that, Sheila said, "Fix it, Sam. You know you need Myra more than Myra needs you." So, I let the CEO go and came back to Myra with my tail between my legs. I think my apology involved some groveling and raising her salary, but we both knew she was worth it. She's been with me now for over a quarter of a century.

In fact, we joke that she has been working for me longer than she's been with both of her husbands combined! She was married when I met her. After she split with that guy, I introduced her to Michael Crawford. It was 2001 and he was working for my racing team, Sam Schmidt Motorsports (more on that later). The two got married in 2005. They are still together today. You can add matchmaker to my many talents. Currently I am four for four when it comes to matchmaking.

I was finally getting settled into a routine at home in Las Vegas, but I was starting to drive Sheila crazy. Previously, I was on the road about 250 days a year, and she had the house to herself. Now I was home all the time. Eventually she asked me what I wanted to do with the rest of my life? She said, "You're driving me nuts. You need to find something to do or else . . . !" So, in 2001 I started the race team and threw myself into it, 150 percent.

For thirty years, Marv's Chevy Only was the place to go for Chevrolet parts in Southern California. My parents, Marv and Judy, are pictured on the far right, along with their dedicated employees.

From an early age, I loved to drive—even Dad's forklift.

My beautiful mom and talented dad with two of his many racing trophies in 1972.

Dad in one of his off-road races. This is similar to what he was racing in 1974, in Mexico, when he was hit and became paralyzed.

Sheila and I were married on November 14, 1992, on a bluff in Palos Verdes that overlooked the ocean. She is my angel and has been the most amazing partner for more than three decades.

This 50cc Honda was my Christmas gift when I was five years old. Circa 1970 at Indian Dunes.

1992: The first time Sheila saw me drive was at Willow Springs International Raceway in Rosamond, California, for one of my SCCA races. I won that day!

When I qualified for my first Indy 500 in 1997, I celebrated with my family on the famous yard of bricks on the front stretch of Indianapolis Motor Speedway. Back row (left to right): Galen Schmidt, Pat and Connie Anderson, my dad Marv, and my mom Judy. Front row (left to right): Me and Sheila.
Credit: IMS Photo

The Indianapolis 500. The Greatest Spectacle in Racing. There is nothing like it. This was in 1999 and was my last time driving an IndyCar at the famed Indianapolis Motor Speedway.
Credit: IMS Photo

When I won the IndyCar race at Las Vegas Motor Speedway in 1999, the Las Vegas newspaper headlines simply said: "Sam's Town." I had dressed up like Elvis that week to promote the race and still had the sideburns when I stood in Victory Lane.
Credit: IMS Photo

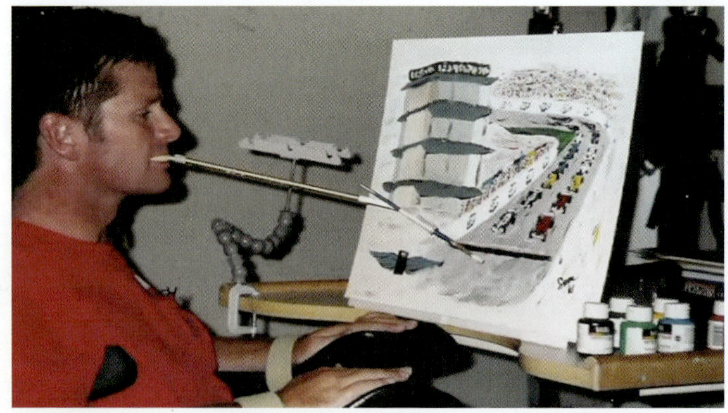

I had fun learning to paint shortly after my accident. It was therapeutic, and, considering I was using my mouth, I think I did OK! But Spencer is the true artist in the family.

Immediately after my accident, I was in St. Louis for rehab. Savannah loved to climb on me, and her innocent little laughs would always brigthen the mood.

It really doesn't look that bad does it? This was the aftermath of the crash in 2000 at Walt Disney World Speedway that changed my life forever.
Credit: IMS Photo

By 2005, we had found our new normal which included riding in the Camaro I restored myself when I was fourteen. I still own the car.

My dad is the reason I got involved in racing. We've enjoyed many memorable days at the racetrack. In 2014, at Indianapolis Motor Speedway, we were all smiles when Simon Pagenaud won the Inaugural Indy Grand Prix.

In 2011, Alex Tagliani, driving for Sam Schmidt Motorsports, earned the pole position for the 95th Running of the Indianapolis 500 Mile Race. It was my first Indy 500 pole position as a team owner and a feeling I will remember forever.

2011 was such a roller-coaster year. I'll always cherish this moment with my family and Dan Wheldon after he won the Indy 500 driving a car we prepared for him. Thanks to Dan, I finally got an Indy 500 winner's ring. Sadly, we lost Dan just a few months later. Losing him was almost unbearable.

Arrow Electronics officially became a naming rights partner to the IndyCar team in 2019.
Credit: Arrow Electronics

Check it out. Thanks to the Arrow Exoskeleton, I am actually taller than Sheila.
Credit: Arrow Electronics

It took a lot of good old-fashioned duct tape but I managed to skydive. Father's Day 2021.

Me doing burnouts at the Indianapolis Motor Speedway in 2016. The RCR4LIF license plate seemed appropriate.
Credit: Arrow Electronics

Sheila, the kids, and I with our guide Dave proving that nothing beats a bluebird day on the slopes in Vail, 2024.

At the Kennedy Space Center, we paused for a photo with *Inspiration*—a fitting name—before going full throttle down the runway. I reached 213 mph that day.
Credit: Arrow Electronics

From driving to dancing, the Arrow Electronics engineering team gave me a way to do things everyone else said I would never do again. I'm forever endebted to these talented and DRIVEN individuals.
Credit: Arrow Electronics

Going Global—In 2022, I drove the McLaren version of the SAM Car in the iconic hill climb at the historic Goodwood Festival of Speed in West Sussex, England.
Credit: Arrow Electronics

Racing up Pikes Peak in 2016 with co-driver Robby Unser was insane. Remember: I was driving with my mouth and head. It was dangerous, challenging, memorable, fun, and never to be repeated.
Credit: Arrow Electronics

My wife and I dancing for the first time in more than twenty years. Our two kids dancing beside us. My parents watching in the background. Deep down, I knew God would allow this moment to happen, and I savored every single second of it!
Credit: Braedon Flynn

Full circle moment! I started my days at the racetrack watching my dad race. Then I was a driver. Then I was an owner. Now I am a Dad watching his son race. I couldn't be more proud!

My driving career was cut short, but my life was not. I have my Vegas winning car in my house as a reminder of that chapter but also as motivation to stay DRIVEN. Getting to stand next to it again (thanks to Arrow) was a dream come true.
Credit: Arrow Electronics

Pepperdine is a special place for our family. Giving a commencement speech (for my son's class) and receiving an honorary doctorate is a dream come true. If I could pinch myself, I would.

12

OUR LITTLE ENGINE(S) THAT COULD

WHILE I WAS WORKING with Myra and she was helping me with everything from my strength and muscle range of motion to booking events, I was building two of the pillars of my new life: the foundation and the racing team.

For the foundation, I wanted to gather a bunch of the brightest minds that I knew from the field of spinal cord injury research. Since we'd already established something in my name, my job now was to grow it to become an organization that could stand on its own merit. Christopher Reeve had already done so much work in the field. He raised millions for research and laid the groundwork. We wanted to continue that work and follow his example. I also had the example of my quadriplegic friend Darrell Gwynn, a drag racer who organized events for spinal cord research, and Formula 1 team owner Sir Frank Williams, who did similar work. During my time in the hospital, I saw just how many layers of need there were, not just for the patients, but also for their families. Rehabilitation, equipment, travel, home modifications—all of it requires time and money. But what hit me hardest was how much the emotional toll extended beyond the injury itself. Families suffer as their lives are turned upside down too, and it can be easy to overlook them in the recovery process.

Some of the team who volunteered to help in addition to my best friend, Jeff Jones, were: Ed Mattix, who ran PR and communications for Sprint PCS out of Kansas City; Don Brooks, who I drove for during the 1995 Hooters series; Todd Davis, who is the cofounder of the identity theft company LifeLock; and Scott Cronk, who was the team manager at Treadway Racing. I also recruited Pat Rummerfield; Kimberly Hobbs from Sprint; and several racing vets, including Fred Treadway, Tom Kelley, Ruthie Culbertson, and Arie Luyendyk. My family was also, of course, pivotal. It was a remarkable group of people who came together with a shared purpose—to help me turn tragedy into something that could help others. Our first major event was held at The Orleans Casino in Las Vegas on April 20, 2001. It was a successful night, but it also was just the beginning.

It was a grind in the early years. The deeper I got into the effort, the more I realized I had *a lot* to learn. One of the first things we observed was that every community has someone like me. Maybe he or she wasn't a racecar driver, but there was someone who had been in an accident or was in need. The community always rallied around them to get them a van or a new wheelchair. The smaller things were being taken care of, but there wasn't enough effort being made for the bigger picture, to raise funds to create real, long-term change. So, we thought, instead of taking care of every community's *individual*, we needed to help solve the problem of paralysis, as a whole. We began researching ways to get funding. An obvious first step seemed to be soliciting my racing contacts. As I've said, the motorsports community is a family, and they know how to rally behind a cause! As the years passed, we were able to allocate more and more money toward research. We established a board of directors and hired a few key staff. We were on our way with the foundation but had much more ground to cover.

* * *

Even though I was no longer able to drive a car, the fire to race had not gone anywhere. I still wanted to compete. I still wanted to win. So, in 2001, only fourteen months after my accident, I announced the formation of Sam Schmidt Motorsports. I couldn't be behind the wheel, but I knew how the racing world worked. I believed I could raise the money, and I knew who I needed to hire to build a team that could compete. I went back to my roots, to my father's work ethic and to not taking "no" for an answer. I leaned into my story because I knew people wanted to help after the accident, to be a part of something bigger. The Indy Racing League, still recovering from its split with CART, needed more cars and strong new owners. Plus, my story was a marketing opportunity they couldn't ignore. What I brought to the table was a $400,000 chassis that I still owned from my former career. That was my starting point.

As I looked for drivers, I sought out guys who were hungry and able to bring some of their own money or sponsors to the table. The team I created was like the Little Engine That Could! I was not bashful about picking up the phone and calling anybody, anywhere, at any time, inquiring about sponsorship or other opportunities. Our budget for our first year was around $1.2 million. We knew that if we finished well, we could make some of it back. While I'd like to say we made money our first year, we probably broke even. A few crashes set our budget back. I grew up in an automotive recycling facility, and I knew how to stretch a dollar, find a part, and hustle. We were streetwise and scrappy. We never turned down a sponsor, even if it was as little as $5,000. If a company helped buy some equipment, they retained the right to earn money back if we ever turned around to sell it. That kind of transparency mattered. We were David and the rest of the racing world was Goliath. My story really set us apart, though. Every city we went to, the local press wanted to talk. We never hurt for media coverage.

My ambition was big, even if our initial budget was not. I wanted our team to become the next Team Penske. Roger Penske made a global conglomerate out of savvy, hard work and racing excellence.

I didn't have his resources or road map, but I had the same drive and belief in what was possible. With that goal, I started in the top tier series of the Indy Racing League.

In the beginning, we were all about the grind. We were frugal because we had to be. Several team members stayed in one hotel room, and we drove to races instead of flying. One thing we never compromised on was preparation. We partnered with LP Racing our first year, which was the team I'd worked with when I was just starting to drive in the Indy Racing Series. Owned by Larry and Lee Anne Nash, their cars were immaculate. We joked that the LP stood for "Let's polish," but sometimes I wonder if that was a joke or reality. One of our goals was to always have our presentation look as good as a Penske car. I remember at one race in Phoenix a crew member from Penske walked by our car, went a few feet more, and then turned around. As he looked at the gearbox, I overheard him say, "I don't think we can do as good as that. This car is absolutely pristine." It was like getting a compliment from the Pope.

I don't want to make it seem like I have the golden touch, because I don't, and I'm no genius. We just worked as hard, if not harder, than anyone else in the paddock. That was my number one rule for the team. That mindset led to some high highs, but racing is still racing and, as I knew all too well, the lows could be devastating.

Our first driver was Davey Hamilton, someone I'd raced against and respected. He'd driven for A. J. Foyt and brought both funding and experience. Most importantly, he still had that drive to win. He only drove five races for us; he was sidelined by a horrific crash at Texas Motor Speedway in June 2001. He suffered significant injuries to his feet and legs. His wreck almost made me get out of the sport for good, before we really even got started. The guy in front of him blew an engine; he had nowhere to go. Davey's car got backward coming off of turn 2 and caught air, which put him into the catch fence. The impact ripped off the front third of his car, which exposed his legs and feet as he slid down the entire length of the back stretch. When he got to the hospital, he was missing most of the soft tissue from his knees down and had no heels left. The doctors in Texas wanted to amputate but luckily, we convinced his family to decline the surgery and get him airlifted to Indianapolis to see the same doctors who treated me after my Texas crash just two years earlier. These doctors had unmatched experience with racing injuries and were able to save Davey's legs. After twenty-one surgeries, he actually returned to racing and finally retired in 2025. Yes, we are a sick group of individuals.

After Davey's crash, we went through a few other drivers trying to find the right combination of chemistry and funding. Richie Hearn, Alex Barron, Anthony Lazzaro, and Jaques Lazier all drove for me. Jaques gave us our first real breakthrough: a pole position at Richmond International Raceway and a podium at Nashville Superspeedway. Like everything, it came at a cost.

Motorsports journalist Marshall Pruett later called the Nashville race one of the "strangest and most emotional" race endings he'd ever seen. Jaques had just secured the team's first podium finish when, just as he crossed the finish line, he lost control and totaled the car. This was only weeks after Davey's accident, and Davey was actually at that race in a wheelchair, his legs in casts. We had our long-awaited podium, and then we had another major crash. Thankfully, Jaques was okay. The prize money evaporated, but the message was clear: People were paying attention to our small team.

In our next race at Kentucky Speedway, we finished twelfth. Then we lost Jaques, our most successful driver, to a team owned by John Menard. If you didn't know by now, racing isn't for the faint of heart, loyalty can be fleeting, and people will do whatever they can to win. Anthony Lazzaro became our fifth and final driver for the season. We finished the year thirteenth overall, lucky thirteen. If I wasn't so damn stubborn, I may have quit right there. Instead, I hung on for a couple more decades.

One of the reasons I stayed was simple: my passion for racing and for the competition. I loved rolling around the garages in my chair, talking with drivers and team members, signing autographs (now, using a pen in my mouth), and just being part of the community. It all gave me purpose; I jumped in with everything I had. I was driven by the desire to win and also to help inspire those who needed it—that's what kept me motivated.

Our second season was just as volatile. Like 2001, for a variety of reasons, we had five different drivers: Mark Dismore, Jimmy Kite, Anthony Lazzaro, Greg Ray, and Richie Hearn. After that year, I knew I needed to adjust my plan. I shifted my focus to find more stability. The Indy Racing League started a feeder series. At the time, it was called the Infiniti Pro Series, and as I am writing this it's called Indy NXT. Despite various rebrands, industry insiders have always known it as "Indy Lights," which is a nod to what it was prior to the CART and IRL split. It offered something the big leagues didn't: a chance to build consistency, develop young talent, and create a foundation for long-term success at a fraction of the cost of the IRL. So, I made the leap. I poured everything I had into turning our team into a dominant force in that series. And over time, that's exactly what we became. Our Indy Lights team eventually would go on to earn seventy-five victories and seven championships, becoming the most successful team in the history of the series to that point. Commentators started calling us the "Penske of Indy Lights." To me, that was the biggest compliment we could have received, and proof that persistence is key.

Like the IRL team, the early years in this series were exhausting, but they laid the foundation for everything that came next. Once we made the move to Indy Lights, things started to click. With a lower budget, more control, and a focus on development, we could finally build something lasting. As the years went on, I was on the road anywhere between 130 and 220 days a year, splitting time between the racetrack and speaking engagements for the foundation. That kind of travel is brutal for anyone, but being paralyzed from the neck down made it a logistical and physical nightmare. Every trip required a nurse, a rigid routine, and an almost military level of preparation just to get through an airport or a hotel stay. And yet, I kept doing it—because the work mattered, and because I refused to be sidelined.

Persistence paid off. In 2004, with driver Thiago Medeiros, we won six races and claimed our first Indy Lights championship. That kicked off a remarkable run. Over the next decade, our team won seven titles with drivers Jay Howard (2006), Alex Lloyd (2007), Jean-Karl Vernay (2010), Josef Newgarden (2011), Tristan Vautier (2012), and Sage Karam (2013).

* * *

I was well on my way to answering Sheila's question about what I was going to do with my life. The race team was hitting its stride, and we were raising hundreds of thousands of dollars annually for the foundation. We started "Day at the Races" events, where dozens of people in wheelchairs and their caregivers get to enjoy a day at the track. They get to meet drivers, team owners, and sponsors. We also lobbied for legislation that would provide funding for stem cell research and oppose cuts in critical public health programs.

Despite the hectic travel schedule I was keeping, I stayed committed to my rehab routine. Fitness for me wasn't optional. It was essential to keep blood flowing and help maintain my immune system. At times, I even let myself feel a little hope: Maybe, just maybe, I would be able to move my arms and legs again one day.

Before I was hurt, I was a professional athlete at the top of my game. Now, I was an ex–IndyCar driver who could make a difference in other ways. It wasn't so bad if I could focus on goals like the race team, the foundation, and walking my daughter down the aisle. It may have been naive to think I could do it all, but I would not let it be for a lack of effort.

If my father didn't blame anyone for his accident and paralysis, then I certainly wasn't going to. As racers, we understand the risks. If I'd gotten hurt sitting at a red light or getting hit by a stray bullet through my drywall, I might not have been able to stay so positive. But my accident happened while I was living my dream. That gave it meaning. From that point on, I had new goals to chase, and I knew I had to give them everything I had left in me.

13

PASSION VS. PURPOSE

IN 2004, my racing team manager, Michael Crawford, was in the Indianapolis Motor Speedway garage area prior to the Indy Lights race when a couple of guys walked up to him and told him they knew a guy who'd like to sponsor our team for the Indy 500. Usually, those kinds of conversations go nowhere, but this one was different. It turned out they were for real. The guys just happened to work for Lucas Oil, and soon after, I was on the phone with Forrest Lucas. He was from Indiana and had always wanted to sponsor a car in the 500, but he never had the resources. This was a win-win. We made a deal within fifteen minutes on the phone, he showed up the next day, and we were inseparable for the next two weeks leading up to the race.

As luck would have it, the night before Michael met them, I had received a call from Tim Cindric, president of Penske Racing. It was early May, and it was looking as if there were only thirty-two cars entered in the race. Historically, there have always been thirty-three entries in the 500 and, well, Roger wanted to make sure there would be this year as well. He was calling to offer our team Gil de Ferran's backup car so we could be in the race. I had to ask him if I was being punked. "Are you freaking kidding me?" He said, "No, I am Tim Cindric." I responded, "Absolutely!" before he could change his mind. I had no idea how our Indy Lights team would facilitate it, but this was an opportunity that I could not turn down. As it turned out, Team Penske would not only provide the car, but also the engine lease, a full set of pit lane equipment used by its test team, and personnel to operate it. I could not have planned for it to work out any better if I had tried.

Now, if I only knew a driver who could get up to speed quickly at the Brickyard. We had already missed the first week of practice and qualifying. It just so happens that I did: Richie Hearn. I called him right after I got off the phone with Tim. He was at the airport an hour later and took the red-eye to Indy. That is what true race-car drivers are willing to do just for the opportunity to drive in the Indy 500. Within twenty-four hours, we had a car, an engine lease, pit lane equipment, extra manpower, and a one-race sponsor all for the *Greatest Spectacle in Racing.* Although the help from Penske was critical, the sponsorship with Forrest Lucas became a game changer. What started as a one-off deal quickly evolved into an ongoing partnership. Forrest became a mentor, close friend, and believer in what we were trying to build. He played a major role in helping us grow the team. That's how it happened: a couple of guys walked up to Michael, and we became regular Indy 500 participants and partners with Lucas Oil for over twenty-five years. But it was the personal relationships with Forrest and his wife, Charlotte, as well as their son, Morgan, and his wife, Katie, that mattered to me the most. It was proof that in racing integrity and treating people the right way can change everything.

In the 2004 Indy 500, Richie started in the thirtieth position but drove a smart, steady race and fought all the way up to finish twentieth. Not too shabby. Everyone ended the day proud of what we accomplished in such a short time. For me, just being there wasn't enough. I wasn't driving anymore, but I still had a burning desire to win the Indy 500.

Even as we worked toward our racing goals, I was still adjusting to the realities of my new life, some big and others, surprisingly, small. When you experience a major life change like paralysis, it can be easier to focus on the big-picture stuff, adjusting goals and ambitions. You rally for yourself and your family. You can redesign your house with ramps, wider doors, and roll-in showers. It is the little, everyday details that often catch you off guard. When people ask me what the hardest part of being a quadriplegic is, one of the first things that always comes to mind is those moments in the middle of the night when I wake up with an idea for something new. Most people can roll over, grab a pen or a phone, and jot something down. I can't do that. If inspiration strikes at 3 A.M., I either have to hold on to it in my head or hope I can get someone's attention to help—without letting the thought slip away. It's a small thing, but small things add up.

For me, being paralyzed means having to delegate almost everything. I do everything I can not to let moments of frustration turn into patterns of anger and resentment. Instead, I try to laugh, keep a positive attitude, and stay focused on what I *can* do. The alternative would be too heavy to carry. Sometimes, it can take a devastating moment to teach you how precious life can be. Cynicism comes easy. Hope takes work. The positive way to look at it all is this: I can do so much more now thanks to all the people who are willing to help and all the people who now work *with* me. I still have my mind, my voice, and my drive to make things happen. And trust me, the one part of me that definitely never slowed down is my mouth! I can talk all day long. Sometimes I wish I would sleep more instead of dreaming up more things to do. My assistant, Myra, knows that all too well. Whenever I get a sudden idea—like adding an unscheduled stop or last-minute detour—she just shakes her head. "And when we're late," she says, "Who do you think they blame? Not Sam!"

What keeps me going has changed over time. Early on, it was sheer survival. Later, it developed into purpose—about finding ways to use what I'd experienced and learned to help others. My family and friends have always been my anchor, and my faith has been the quiet, steady force that carried me through the darkest moments.

* * *

As time passed, my new life became more routine, more "normal," both for me and everyone around me. I found purpose in staying busy and said yes to just about every opportunity that gave me a chance to make a difference, whether I thought I could handle it or not. In 2012, a big decision I made that really paid off, not only financially but intrinsically, was investing in and joining the board of BraunAbility, which manufactures and sells wheelchair accessible lifts and vehicles. Founded by Ralph Braun, who was diagnosed with spinal muscular atrophy at six years old, the company has grown year after year for decades now. I had firsthand experience of what those vehicles needed. I'd ridden in vans thousands and thousands of miles. And to this day, Braun's incredible workforce continues to create great products for people with disabilities.

One of the aspects of my life I had to quickly get used to was my own wheelchair. I control it with a device called a "head array" built into the headrest. It has three pads, one on the left, one on the right, and one behind my head. As soon as I get within a quarter of an inch of any of them, the chair senses my head and it moves in that direction. I also have a switch next to one of my cheeks that if I press on it, it will reverse the direction, and I will go forward when I lean my head back. The switch also controls many other functions such as tilt, recline, seat elevator, and speed. My mother liked to make the joke, "That's the first time he's ever used his head to drive anything!" *Har-dee-har-har!*

While my kids loved to climb and play on the chair, it wasn't a toy, though that didn't always stop us from getting into some trouble. For one of my chairs, I had an engineer friend build a step on the back so the kids could ride along with me. In 2004, we took the whole family to a race at the Kansas Speedway. Well, at one point on the trip, I was in the motor home lot at the track, alternating rides with both of the kids. When Savannah got on the step behind me, I popped a wheelie but at the same time turned my head to the right by accident, which turned the entire chair abruptly. It tipped over. Savannah jumped off like an action hero, and I went tumbling. I hit my head on the asphalt and knocked myself out. I woke up to ten people asking me if I was okay as blood trickled from my ear. Sheila and Myra got the chair upright and took me to the medical center at the track. I was worried that Savannah was freaking out about the whole thing and would ultimately have PTSD. Thankfully, the doctor told me that luckily nothing major was wrong, other than a broken pinkie and a scraped-up ear. I still remember Rick Mears—my hero—popping his head into my room and saying, "I told you never to turn right!"

It was moments like that one that reminded me to take better care of my wheelchair. The headrest alone costs about $5,000 and the chair, which weighs about four hundred pounds, costs another $25,000. It's an expensive beast. Insurance pays for the base model, but they don't reimburse for modifications that make it truly functional, like a seat elevator that lets me look people in the eye as I'm talking to them or rise up in a photo. I wish insurance companies were better partners, more dependable and willing to understand what real independence requires.

I'm grateful that I had the help I needed in other areas of my life to ensure that I stay on top of my health, but it has never been simple. One of the biggest risks is staying stationary too long and getting pressure sores. I had one while writing this book that lasted more than ten months. Thanks to people like Myra, Sheila, and others, I went decades without ever developing them. That is unheard of, especially for someone who is upright in a chair as long as I am every day. Even when I go to sleep, I need a plan. One night, I'll sleep on one side of my body. The next night it will be another. I rotate throughout the week so that my body isn't in the same position night after night. I also have about a dozen pillows put around me for support, and they need to be rotated so that they don't cause sores either. Then each morning, I go through my exercises and electronic stimulation to awaken and stretch as many muscles as I can.

* * *

For eleven years, I worked hard at our Indy Lights team. Then in 2011, I had an amazing opportunity to purchase the entire FAAZT IndyCar team. So I decided to return full-time to the major leagues. I thought, *What the hell? Let's try it again.* If we didn't do well, we could always go back to Indy Lights. It didn't take long to get a taste for what our future might hold. On May 21, 2011, with Alex Tagliani behind the wheel, we won the pole position for the Indy 500 on our very first attempt as a team. We were starting first at the biggest race on Earth! It is hard to explain how special it is to start on the pole at Indy. There is so much hype and promotion around that race. Qualifying first at any race is important, but getting the fastest time at Indy is a completely different experience.

The polesitter is instantly thrown into press conferences, national media tours, parades . . . It is a massive multiday celebration leading up to race day. Five years later, we were blessed to experience it all over again when James Hinchcliffe earned the pole.

Despite starting first, our 2011 Indy 500 wasn't the best. After a series of unfortunate events during the race, Alex finished the race twenty-eighth. Our other two drivers, Townsend Bell and Jay Howard, crashed and finished twenty-sixth and thirtieth, respectively. On a much brighter side, I owned, and our team prepared, the chassis for the race winner, the late Dan Wheldon. So I was given a winner's ring for the 2011 Indianapolis 500. Even though Sam Schmidt Motorsports didn't win, I had a taste of victory. It was a tremendous feeling and one I've been chasing ever since.

Pain and struggle were never far away. It got to the point where I felt like we were cursed. On September 12, 2011, the Sam Schmidt Motorsports Indy Lights team manager, Chris Griffis, died suddenly at just forty-six years old. For me personally, Chris was the brother I never had—steady, brilliant, and loyal. Then, just a month later, at the season finale, Dan Wheldon was involved in a horrific fifteen-car accident. He died at my home track, Las Vegas Motor Speedway, while driving the No. 77 car, jointly owned by Bryan Herta Autosport and our team. It went airborne and when he hit the fence, he was killed instantly. We lost one of the most charismatic and gifted drivers in the racing community. Dan was a champion on and off the track—a devoted husband, father, and friend whose smile could light up the paddock. We all know the risks we take as drivers and racing team owners, but that doesn't make any of these difficult times easier. In dark hours, I wondered why I survived and Dan didn't. I also knew that wasn't a road I could let myself go down. There is no light at the end of that tunnel. All I could do is honor his memory by carrying on and trying to make the sport worthy of his legacy.

In 2012, we renamed our team Schmidt Hamilton Motorsports after Davey Hamilton secured a primary sponsorship with HP, which is what we needed to continue racing IndyCar full time. Our driver, Simon Pagenaud, won the IndyCar Rookie of the Year Award after garnering four podiums that year. In 2013, we changed names again when Ric Peterson bought a stake in the team; we became Schmidt Peterson Motorsports. Simon was still driving for us, and we finished third in the series point standings. Over the years, on top of our two Indy 500 poles, we won several IndyCar races. *Our Little Engine That Could* was now a *Big Engine That Did.*

While building the IndyCar team, we had still been running our Indy Lights team. It had been a successful thirteen-year run, but, at the end of the 2016 season, we decided to end our Indy Lights program to focus on our IndyCar team and that elusive Indy 500 win. I had fantastic team members, but I just couldn't handle the pressure of overseeing both operations.

Around the same time, we decided to rebrand the Sam Schmidt Paralysis Foundation. We had grown into a multimillion-dollar organization. In 2015, we wanted to stress our mission of trying to find a cure for paralysis, so we changed the organization's name to Conquer Paralysis Now (CPN). Our focus continued in the same way it always had—providing grants to major research at places like Georgetown University School of Medicine; University of California at Irvine; Columbia University; the Mayo Clinic; Salk Institute for Biological Studies; raising money for spinal cord injury research; hosting our regular Day at the Races events; lobbying with lawmakers in Washington and inspiring people (and their families) to take back their lives post-injury. However, the hope with the new name was to make our mission clearer to the public. Ultimately, we have one goal. I believe, more than ever, that with a hundred million dollars in resources, we can transform the system in a decade—providing more independence, mobility, and hope to people with paralysis than ever before. A cure doesn't look the same for everyone, but with the right funding and focus, we can change countless lives. The *cure* for paralysis is only a matter of time and money. We will get there. We'll find it. Our best years are ahead of us. *It's not if, but when!*

In December 2018, we began to realize our full potential with the opening of the first DRIVEN Neuro Recovery Center in downtown Las Vegas. The facility provides the kind of activity-based therapy that I do myself every day, the same kind of therapy that Dr. Sadowsky and Dr. McDonald touted in St. Louis when I was first injured. It's also an open gym, a yoga facility, and a community center. It offers a number of other services, from mental health support to education resources. On the rehabilitation side of things, we have state-of-the-art equipment that help retrain people to walk again, continuing to strengthen the muscles that they need to walk so that their body never forgets and that their muscles do not atrophy too much. The best part is that we offer all of this to our customers regardless of insurance or financial limitations.

Today, my dream is for every person suffering with a neurological disability to have access to DRIVEN or a facility like it, where they can rebuild their strength, independence, and confidence. Over the two and a half decades, our foundation has raised tens of millions of dollars to advance research and bring hope to those living with paralysis. We still sponsor research projects and other initiatives, but establishing more DRIVEN facilities has become the organization's central mission. We do this not only for those recently injured or diagnosed, but also for the millions of Americans who have been living with neurological disorders for many years. I believe this purpose is why I am still here today.

The DRIVEN mission is to provide intensive rehabilitation and support in a controlled environment. Spinal cord injuries happen every day in America because of car accidents, sports injuries, falls, or other traumatic accidents. They occur usually when fragments of bone tear into the spinal cord and disrupt the nerves that carry signals from the brain to the rest of the body. Neurological issues can also occur from cancer, arthritis, or osteoporosis. There are many kinds of spinal cord injuries, and they can cause full or partial paralysis. We also see clients who have neurological conditions due to strokes, Multiple Sclerosis (MS), combat injuries, or Amyotrophic Lateral Sclerosis (ALS), also known as Lou Gehrig's disease. DRIVEN offers the services that all these people depend on. If you're a quadriplegic, your life in many ways depends on you keeping your muscles active so that they stay strong and capable of metabolically processing things like sugars. If you don't work out, your muscles atrophy and turn into fat. You have to have an athlete's state of mind. Millions of people are suffering from these conditions, and we want to help heal them and give them a new sense of purpose in the world. Just like the foundation has given me.

As time passed, I learned just how deep the rabbit hole goes. For one thing, spinal cord injuries are extremely complex and there are many kinds that can affect people differently. Secondly, deciding which research to fund is really difficult, especially as most of the studies were making very little progress until about 2018. I interviewed some researchers who we considered partnering with who had been working away for some twenty-five years and I thought, *Why would I want to work with you if you've solved nothing in that much time?* Sadly, I learned that some in the field aren't always motivated by results, they just want to sustain their labs and maintain a regular paycheck. Half-measures only burn money and that is not what we wanted to incentivize. Early on, we tried to model our funding strategy after Christopher Reeve's foundation, but it quickly became clear that we needed to chart our own path because I wanted to see more aggressive, innovative solutions that were not available at the time.

Our team stayed small and lean, but grew in calculated, incremental steps. Early on, I even went to Congress to testify about the benefit of stem cell research. However, at the end of the day, I realized that dealing with politicians was not for me. I now have friends who have the patience to deal with the chaos of federal lobbying. To me, it felt like if you aren't bringing them a sack of cash for their campaign or a boatload of votes, all they give you is lip service. On one occasion, I had a heated discussion with a senator who was vehemently against stem cell research. It is a long story, but I left truly feeling like it was a waste of my time. I also got a solid hour with Barack Obama when he was a senator. He knows how to make you feel like you are the most important person in the room. After two trips visiting Congress in 2002 and 2005, I learned I just didn't have the patience for it and said I was never going back. I deeply admire those who do have the tolerance to work with elected officials, and I also respect the work our government officials do. We need everyone coming together to help, but I needed to focus my attention on faster solutions. So, I pivoted from DC, and I doubled down on my fundraising tactics and the research opportunities. All the while, the need for our DRIVEN facilities became clearer.

The major epiphany came when I opened my eyes to the reality that Las Vegas, the city I called home, was desperately lacking in critical medical facilities. There's a lot to love about the city, from the low taxes and access to entertainment to the corporate environment and the weather, but the joke for a long time in Vegas has been, "If you need serious medical attention, go to the airport so you can fly somewhere else." It was only a few years ago that UNLV opened its medical school, but there are few places in the city for its graduates to work. This will change in time, but for now, the city is something of a medical desert. So we knew we had to help. We want to be part of the *solution*, not just complain about it.

We wanted to do something different. We wanted to admit *all* people. We wanted to offer physical assistance as well as mental health counseling, even marriage and family counseling. So, we leased a 7,500 square-foot building downtown and renovated it. The place is thirty minutes from anywhere in the city and in close proximity to public transportation. Suddenly, we had our new direction. We opened our doors and thanks to our foundation supporters, as well as our incredible team members, DRIVEN was officially born. Now, my mantra is *Racing is my passion; DRIVEN is my purpose.*

* * *

About five years ago, I looked at the list of drivers at the Indy 500, and I noticed that thirteen had raced for Sam Schmidt Motorsports. That was a pivotal moment of reflection for me. We've done well over the years, but more than trophies or prize money, our claim to fame is to have helped build the careers of some of the world's best drivers. I had a unique leadership style because I was a businessman and a driver, but I didn't have a specific strategy when we started the team. We just put one foot in front of the other and did the next right thing. We tried to do the most we could with what we had. I have always tried to have the utmost integrity and to lead by example.

It's all about what you can control. For example, in my everyday life, I know that when people who don't know me see me in my chair, they don't understand what I can do. Sometimes, I'll roll into a car dealership with Spencer or Savannah, and we'll just sit there and no one will help me. They don't know that I work with the best automobiles in the world. They just see someone in a chair who they believe will never drive again. I can't fault them for that, but I also can't let it get me down. I still go out with family and friends regularly. At restaurants, I'll take bites off other people's plates and ask for sips of their drinks. You have to define your own life. Really, the only low days I have are when people on my staff let me down. All I've ever asked of anybody is to do what they say they will do, and to do it in a timely manner. I don't ask anything of them that I don't ask of myself from a commitment standpoint. And they are getting paid.

Over the years, accidents like mine have led to many changes in the racing world. For example, the material used to make race-car seats (and other foam bead products) has substantially evolved since my accident. It had been made of Styrofoam that was hard as cement, but the manufacturers of the foam changed the composition after I was hurt. Now, it's more forgiving and won't damage the spine upon impact. The George family, who used to own the IRL and the Indianapolis Motor Speedway, also improved other measures for racers, including developing the SAFER barrier that has now been adopted by all types of motorsports facilities around the world. My accident shook up the spinal cord injury field in the same way that it did when Christopher Reeve was injured. Christopher brought the spotlight, but I helped keep the light on. And in 2013, that was underscored yet again after I received a phone call that would change my life forever.

14

PROJECT S.A.M.

SERENDIPITY is a marvelous, unpredictable thing. I got an unexpected call in 2013, and it changed my life. One single phone call gave me a new sense of freedom that I never thought I would ever feel again. I almost didn't even answer it because it was a number that was not in my phone. Boy, am I glad I did. On the other end of the phone was Joe Verrengia, the senior director of marketing and global head of brand for Arrow Electronics. He told me about their revolutionary idea to create an experimental car that could be driven without hands or legs. Then he said six simple words: "We want you to drive it."

After the call, I turned to Sheila and said, "Hey, how would you feel about me driving again?" She rolled her eyes. I admit I wasn't certain about it either, but I also couldn't deny the feeling of hope in my gut. The first good sign was that Joe didn't ask for money. Sheila left it up to me if I wanted to talk more with them, but she wasn't exactly thrilled about the idea of me driving again. "So much could go wrong," she said. She was right. Plus, it seemed like a pipe dream that I'd ever get behind the wheel again. But I couldn't throw the chance away, could I? It wasn't exactly a calm season of my life. The foundation, the racing team, BraunAbility, the upcoming Indy 500—I was on the road more than ever. But to drive again? To be behind the wheel of a car? If there was even a slight possibility that it would work, I was ready to give it a go. I had to know more. I told Sheila it couldn't hurt to listen, so I decided to meet with the Arrow team.

Given my profile and situation, there have been plenty of people who have approached me with crazy ideas that they wanted me to promote, various technologies to "improve my life" or "give me more independence." Few, if any, prior to this seemed worth my time and energy. Most of the time, you'd plug the device in and then wonder what was so good about it. Honestly, the only thing that has really improved my independence to a measurable degree has been Alexa and Siri. They help me look up something online, turn on electronic devices for me, or call Sheila when I need her. But Joe and Arrow Electronics were different. From the first conversation, I knew this had potential.

While some might think I would want to be on a beach somewhere relaxing in my later years, I was the opposite. I wanted to dive into more work. Sheila will tell you she didn't marry a beach bum. It wasn't because we needed the money or because I didn't have a loving family at home. I just *needed* to work. To stay busy. To help people. To drive again!

Freedom isn't found through laziness. Sheila believes no one should have to sit at home and do nothing because of their situation, diagnosis, or condition. And she's right. That's what I tell people who I talk to in hospitals. The goal isn't to sit at home with a bottle of beer watching ESPN—there's no cure or salvation there. It's to get out and live your life. How else do you get to the next day if you don't have hope, dreams, and direction for the future? You have to find your passion and move forward. Some people thought I was crazy to want to drive again, but I've been racing since I was five years old. It's all I've ever truly wanted to do.

In the years since my accident, I had never once envisioned myself behind the wheel of a racecar again. It wasn't that I lost the fire, it's just that there was never a car made for me.

* * *

Arrow Electronics, which was founded in 1935 in New York City, began as a distributor of electronics products. In 2009, CEO Mike Long took over the leadership of the company, which then already boasted thousands of employees. That marked the continuation of the multibillion-dollar company's growth in electronics. The business was doing great, but they were still an unknown brand. That changed after we got together.

Joe, who was originally from Boston, was hired by Arrow to start a corporate social responsibility program. Previously, he'd worked as a science journalist for the Associated Press, so he knew how to tell a story. At the time, Arrow was transitioning from what Joe, a former English major, calls a "supermarket of components" that could be engineered or reengineered for any number of tasks to a full-service solutions company—almost like they were moving from salvage yard to full-service automotive superstore. To get the word out about that switch and their promise of technology providing a better tomorrow for the masses, they needed to shed their anonymity. So, why not hire a quadriplegic racecar driver to drive previously untested technology? Sign me up!

It helped that Mike Long was a huge car guy who owned a collection of hot rods himself and was trying to get more and more into the automotive industry. Mike grew up in Indiana and loved football, horses, and IndyCar. Racing is a technology-driven sport. Cars are loaded with all sorts of tech and electronics. And while Joe didn't know one thing about the sport, he knew Mike wanted to get into it somehow. Mike also suffered some pretty serious injuries as a result of playing football, so he was sensitive to the idea of technology helping people overcome physical impairments. It broadened his view of disability and how technology could be so useful. He told Joe, "I believe technology is going to help people in the future, so figure out a way we can be part of that now." It was just the kind of challenge Joe was looking for.

To begin the new endeavor, Joe attended Arrow's annual conference with the company's engineers. There, he pitched the idea. Out of the roughly 1,500 North American–based engineers, eight signed up. They got to work outlining the next steps, and one of the first jobs was to name the project. Keep in mind, this was before anyone at Arrow knew my name. They landed on "Semi-Autonomous Mobility," or the "SAM car." Like I said, serendipity is an incredible thing! Another key distinction Joe's team made was that whatever they invented wasn't going to be an official medical device, so there was no FDA approval necessary. It all depended on the subject's willingness to take a risk. I guess they found the right guy for that!

Next, they needed a driver. And how did they find me? Prior to ever meeting anyone at Arrow, I used to make it a point to visit hospitals on race weekends in cities where we were racing. When we were in Denver, I would often visit Craig Hospital, one of the nation's leading neurological rehabilitation centers, to talk to patients and look for new treatments. So, when the folks at Arrow were calling around to various places wondering if there happened to be a quadriplegic interested in taking a risk on a new idea, the good people at Craig gave them my number. That's when the phone call came in and that's when I decided to dive in headfirst (as usual). *If they can build it, I can drive it.*

When they found out about me—a former racecar driver who couldn't use his hands or his legs—they knew they had found their perfect test pilot. They flew to Las Vegas in August 2013, and we met at my house. I told Joe lots of people had come to me with ideas and few, if any, ever amounted to anything. I said, "I've never heard of Arrow before, but I looked you guys up and you're pretty big." Then Joe, to his credit, said, "I've never heard of you, either. But I looked you up and you're pretty good!" And that was it. We were pals from then on.

After that meeting, I got more excited about the possibilities. I started to feel like a forty-nine-year-old kid on Christmas morning. When they left, Sheila, always my voice of reason, asked me why I would want to drive again after getting hurt. But I told her I didn't have time to think about the past. *There's a reason the windshield is bigger than the rearview mirror.*

At first, I thought the Arrow team might be out of their minds. I'm a high-level quadriplegic. I can't move anything below my neck, meaning I don't have trunk control and can't sit upright in a chair without help. The idea of me driving a car again, let alone on a racetrack, sounded like pure fantasy. As they explained their vision more, though, I started to believe there was a chance I could actually do this. It quickly became the only thing I could think about.

It also helped that I felt a connection with the CEO. Mike and I had a few beers together in Denver one day, and he was enthusiastic about the project. Not only that, but Mike wanted Sheila on board. He told me he didn't want just my approval; he wanted hers as well. Sheila told him she was in to see where this could go, and so we made it official. "A few years later," Mike says, "I asked Sheila why she said yes so fast, and she said, 'Because I didn't think you could do it!'" *Ha!* I would also like to say that I, too, would never do anything without Sheila's permission, but anyone who knows me would know that is not true. *Better to beg for forgiveness, than ask permission . . .*

The true icing on the cake was our shared goal of showcasing the car at the 2014 Indy 500—the biggest sporting event in the world, complete with some 300,000 spectators. That was our deadline. While we all wanted the car to be good, we knew that if we introduced it at the 500, it would make global headlines. So we got to work. Mike put no budget constraints on us. He just wanted everything to be ready by May 1. "That's your budget!" he said.

The system that I would use to control the car was ingenious. Using a tube in my mouth, I would blow to accelerate and suck to apply the brakes and slow down. A special hat sensed if I moved my head left or right and the car would turn along with me. Early iterations of the car required complete darkness so that light wouldn't interfere with the cameras. To test the technology, we started in simulators. In those first sessions, as I started to use the equipment, I was speechless. If you know me, you know how rare that is!

I had one request of Arrow above and beyond everything else. Safety, you say? Heck no! I told them we *must* go over a hundred miles per hour. I knew that we wouldn't get the attention from the racing community or the media if we were driving forty miles per hour. Plus, I wanted performance; *slow* is not in my vocabulary. We had to push the limits, but, of course, we kept safety in mind. There were a lot of reasons not to go ahead with the Arrow project, but sometimes you just have to go against better judgment. Truth be told, that's what professional racing is all about, especially from a business perspective.

Arrow gave me the freedom to pick the car—within reason, of course—and I didn't hesitate. I chose a 2014 Chevrolet Corvette (C7) Stingray because I knew it would be iconic at the Indy 500. It was also a nod to my dad's old business, and nothing is more American than a Corvette. As we worked together, we went through all of the steps to make our vehicle better, from the handling of the car to the controls to the speed. To get me into it, I had to be dropped into the front seat with a harness. In later stages we ditched the hat with the sensors for glasses with smaller beacons on them for increased accuracy. Everything was integrated into the car's original operating systems. Almost more importantly, for style points, we developed the system enough to drive with the roof removed and the windows down. After all, you can't drive up and down the Las Vegas strip with the top on.

With each passing day, we saw more of the possibilities of what this technology could mean for the rest of the world: recreational driving, farming, medical devices, and much more. A myriad of other industries could learn from what we were doing. We could inspire millions just by taking the car on tour.

The best thing about partnering with Arrow was getting a piece of myself back. For fifteen years, I hadn't been able to do a single thing entirely on my own. I couldn't walk, feed myself, or even scratch an itch without help. Every moment of every day depended on someone else. Then, suddenly, I was able to drive again—I never thought I'd utter those words after my accident. I was able to feel in control of my life and myself for the first time in so long. Eventually, we were able to go not only a hundred miles per hour, but over two hundred. That changed me and much of my perspective on what is possible. I felt a sense of accomplishment and emotional joy that I'd also thought was gone forever. I felt like Sam Schmidt again, thanks to Joe, Mike, and the incredible people at Arrow.

* * *

Arrow engineers began developing the car in Indianapolis. They flew back and forth from Denver, and I would make trips there from Las Vegas. In our first year, we worked with Ball Aerospace & Technologies on the car. They were already a customer of Arrow's and they wanted to help. We also worked with the US Air Force research lab, borrowing software they'd developed with Arrow years before. Mike helped make all those connections. One group that didn't jump on board, though, was Chevrolet (instead of them donating a car, Joe bought one off the lot with a credit card!). They thought it was too risky. Too bad for them; that Corvette would go on to make history.

Five months before Indy, the engineers at Arrow put the new Corvette on a lift in a garage to examine it for the very first time. At that point, they'd created all the necessary apparatuses for the car, but they hadn't installed them on the car yet. All the engineers stood around it, stroking their chins saying, "Hmmm" and "Ohhhh." as if to say, "We have no idea where we are going to put the equipment." Joe took one look and said, "We're dead!" But to everyone's credit, they pulled it together. It was like that movie *Apollo 13*—a group of problem solvers using what we had to get the job done. And boy did they get it done!

What we came up with then seems almost primitive compared to what we have now. I actually can't believe we drove *that* fast with *that* equipment! There were four infrared cameras in the cockpit pointing at the driver's head. They didn't even have a true helmet equipped with sensors at the time—we used a Sam Schmidt Motorsports baseball hat! But those cameras measured the angle of reflection and the computer in the car averaged the four cameras' input and that is what allowed the car to turn. It was instantaneous. To accelerate the car at first, I tilted my head back. It was almost like my head was the gear shift. We soon fixed that. To brake, I bit down on a plate in my mouth—this was even before we developed the sip-and-puff method, which works much better.

As the Indy 500 approached, we weren't sure if we were going to make it, but at the same time we knew we had to deliver. Leading up to May, the Arrow team pulled all-nighters, and Joe pulled every string he could to get the Corvette ready. When I think back to that team of people, it is really a remarkable example of what can be accomplished when everyone is invested in the outcome. The Arrow employees didn't get paid to work on the SAM car. They had regular day jobs and basically worked on this as a side project for free. You wouldn't know it, though. They were all in. Every person felt like it was Indy or bust.

After just nine months, from that first meeting at my house in August 2013 to race week at the Speedway in May 2014, we built something that worked, something that mattered. It wasn't just a car anymore. It was proof of what vision, collaboration, and determination could create.

About a month before we were set to run at Indy, we went out to the Speedway for a test run. The stands were empty. It was cold and raining. Because of my injury, I couldn't feel the temperature or regulate my own, so people had to keep me warm. With the car on the track, they took the roof off, and the team got me in a harness and lowered me into the car like a sack of potatoes. They secured me in the driver's seat, putting Styrofoam bolsters all around me so I couldn't slip one way or the other. It was all pretty crude, but it was a first step. Truly, I'm convinced that Arrow did more in about six months than any other institution could have done in years. It is a testament to the talent they attract. From Noel Marshall to Grace Doepker to Josh Willis, we had many brilliant and dedicated engineers touch this project.

The head of Chevy Racing, Jim Campbell, was there (we invited the company to see our progress), as was the head of the Indianapolis Motor Speedway, Doug Boles. Chevy was stunned we got the car built so quickly. There was concern at first about the rain. We joked we'd get hit by lightning. Everyone thought it was risky. Finally, Joe said, "Gimme the keys." He was ready to drive the thing to show the progress we'd made. We had to get on-track data for the engineers, and we couldn't wait for the perfect environment. I didn't want to wait any longer either. I wanted to feel that *control* again. I felt like an astronaut about to launch into space; I was so excited. I said I was ready to go.

That day, we made it around the first lap at the Speedway at about forty miles per hour despite a few minor technical difficulties. I came back in and told Joe, "It feels great." Sheila and the kids were there, too. I could see the pride in their eyes, and even a few tears of joy. Of course I wanted to go *faster.* It was strange running on the Speedway with no fans. No place feels lonelier than a big empty racetrack. Nevertheless, it was an important and successful test run, and the team felt better. We were full steam ahead for a run in front of fans a month later at the Speedway.

* * *

Joe was always worried about safety, so Arrow equipped the car with a geofence that acted as digital guardrails, meaning that if the car got too close to the walls on the track, it would automatically brake. They understandably didn't want to see me get into an accident. I understood that, but after our first practice run at the Indianapolis Motor Speedway, I told them they had to take that feature out. It was too much of a hindrance. I wanted to get right up against the wall like racecar drivers do, which was closer than six inches. "We don't want you to hit the wall," Joe said. "As a friend and as a brand, I don't want you to die in the car." But I replied, "What's the worst thing that's going to happen to me? Take it off." So the Arrow engineers did. They had to let me be a racecar driver. That was the whole point of the project. I can't believe they agreed.

The funny thing was there was no contract between Arrow and me, no written agreement. There never has been one. We didn't even shake hands, because . . . well . . . I couldn't. I didn't sign any waivers, despite Arrow's risk manager expressing worry over what could happen to me. Arrow doesn't pay me for any of my work or driving. It's a gentleman's agreement and a pure and simple desire to work together. And I'm grateful for it.

When it was time for the month of May, officials said we could run the car as part of the lead-up to Qualification Day, one week before the Indy 500. We were the first car on the track prior to the IndyCar qualifying session. Because I never *officially* retired—I just got hurt and stopped racing—they treated me *like* a competing professional. It was almost indescribable. When I was done and back on pit lane, all the drivers from other teams ran over to me, and there wasn't a dry eye in sight. Joe said that was the hardest he ever cried. By the time I crossed the finish line, the 100,000-plus fans in the stands were amped up. And news of the drive brought in hundreds of thousands of social media views, too. It was a job well done!

While we didn't crack a hundred miles per hour in the Qualification Day run, Monday morning after the Indy 500, track officials let us back on the track and that's when we crossed that all-important barrier—106! We did it, even if the car shook a little in the process. We achieved the goal we set out to hit. And while driver Simon

Pagenaud finished twelfth in the race for Schmidt Peterson Motorsports, the story for us that weekend was the SAM car. There were some 1,200 registered media members at the Indy 500 and just about every one of them wrote about what we pulled off. Everybody wanted to talk to me. There were articles and video stories everywhere. Arrow was pleased, and I was over the moon. It was a game changer for everyone involved. We made a Super Bowl commercial advertising our partnership. *We'd arrived.* It was the first time in a decade and a half that I felt *normal.* And I knew we could do more.

15

NOT IF, BUT WHEN

AFTER OUR SUCCESS at the 2014 Indy 500, we knew we still weren't done. The SAM car proved what was possible, but now we needed to make it better, faster, and easier to drive. We went through a few options to improve the functionality and eventually landed on the "sip-and-puff" method for accelerating and braking. It is technology used in some electric wheelchairs, and it has worked well for us ever since. We also changed the steering methods on the car, and we continue to make more adjustments, as needed, for increased safety and precision. For example, we have a version of the car where I drive on the passenger side, and a co-driver is sitting in the driver's seat. They can take the car over if anything goes wrong. When we were focused on reaching two hundred miles per hour, it was essential to have a co-driver there in case something happened to me.

If I can say one thing about Arrow—beyond the technical abilities—the group genuinely cares. Over the years, we've become friends and partners. They even became title sponsor of my IndyCar team. In 2019, we renamed the organization Arrow Schmidt Peterson Motorsports. Regardless of the project, they never coddled me. We bust each other's chops and share in the emotional wins as much as the technological advancements. We all dedicated a piece of our lives to this, and it created a powerful bond.

There was no need to stop. We kept going. Over the next several years, Mike, the team, and I put up a lot of challenges, and we met or exceeded them all. We broke the two-hundred-miles-per-hour barrier, took the car to several famous tracks, including the Long Beach Street Course, the Sonoma Raceway road course, and even showcased the car on ESPN's *Sports Science* show. In 2016, *Business Insider* awarded it Car Technology of the Year. Together, we proved that with enough drive you can accomplish what most people think is impossible.

My partnership with Arrow led to many *firsts*. In my previous driving career, I worked to win on the track, now our team was making global history with groundbreaking achievements. After driving the SAM car at the Indianapolis Motor Speedway, our next *first* came in 2016 when I earned a street legal driver's license. Initially, we looked to get the license in Colorado, since that's where Arrow was based. But the state, let's just say, was not interested. Then we made a call to some officials in Nevada, and they were very much into the idea. Nevada had just authorized a massive tax rebate to EV car manufacturers, and they were looking to support more new technologies, including the type that our Arrow team was working on. So they knew that partnering with us would only help their growth efforts.

To secure the state's (and world's) first semi-autonomous license, I waited in line at the DMV with teenagers and everyone else. Just like anyone looking to get a license, I had to drive an instructor around town in the SAM car. At one point, Joe pulled a prank and had local law enforcement pull me over. When the officer came up to the window, I told her that yes indeed I did have a license, but it was in my back pants pocket and given my condition, she would need to get it. That one got a good laugh. All jokes aside, I am probably the safest person on the road. Everyone else has coffee or their cell phones or something else in their hands as they're driving. My eyes literally cannot leave the road. Once the testing was done, I officially had a Nevada driver's license—the first and only one for such a high-level quadriplegic in the world. As proud as I was, driving on the street wasn't what I missed. Racing was. So, soon after getting the new license, we looked for more challenges that involved speed.

In June 2016, we decided to take on the treacherous Pikes Peak International Hill Climb in Colorado. The idea came to us through Mike Long. His fishing buddy, businessman Phil Anschutz, had just bought the Broadmoor Hotel and that included ownership of the Hill Climb event. Phil asked Mike, "Don't you have a funky car you're working on? Why don't you bring it up and see how it handles? You can be the pace car for the race." So, Mike called me and asked if I was interested. "Well, hot damn! Of course I am!" I told him. I had never driven the event, but it had always been a lifelong dream. I figured he was talking about a year from now, as I thought there was a lot we would need to do to prepare. Mike had confidence in the car, though, and he convinced us that we were ready. Having our backs up against the wall is the easiest way to get something going. *What did I just get myself into?* I suddenly remembered that over its one-hundred-year history, some fifty or sixty people had died competing in the event. The Pikes Peak track measures 12.42 miles and has 156 turns, climbing 4,720 feet to reach the 14,000-foot summit. There was no margin for error on the track. Despite the danger, I went into the challenge with open eyes and a hopeful mind. If my driving skills and the SAM car could handle those twists and turns, we knew we could do anything. By that point, Arrow and I had gone through many iterations of the Corvette with various versions of the technology. Every time we drove the car, we learned something new. Sometimes we had to push the limits to see where our boundaries were. Pikes Peak would be the most daunting challenge yet.

During practice runs, there was snow everywhere. The climb is gorgeous, but when you're racing up it, you have no time to take in the views. There are few guardrails and plenty of opportunities to make a mistake and even drive off the side. When you're driving it, the tendency is to look way ahead, which requires turning your head. In the SAM car, I couldn't do that because turning my head would turn the actual car. I wasn't scared about the idea of driving the course, but that may have been simple naivety. The course officials only let you practice on the bottom half, so I prepared using a simulator. I managed to get up the virtual track in about fifteen minutes. If I crashed on the computer though, I just had to push the reset button. On the actual hill, you only have one shot.

Up until this point of the project, each Arrow engineer and several executives regularly volunteered to ride with me in the SAM car. For some reason, when we brought up Pikes Peak, nobody raised their hand. Thanks for the confidence, team! That's when fate intervened, *again*. I happened to run into Robby Unser and Al Unser Jr. at the weeklong Performance Racing Industry trade show in Indy. I immediately told them about our plans for the Pikes Peak climb. Al laughed and walked away. Robby had won the event nine times and knew every inch of the hill climb. He immediately agreed to help; you couldn't make this stuff up if you tried. The Unser family is one of the most decorated in all of racing and to have Robby on board changed everything. He understood both the limitations of the technology and the racing mentality that I would bring to the challenge. In that way, Robby and I shared the racer's DNA that I didn't have with anyone else on the Arrow team. Robby and I didn't think about the risks, instead we thought about how fast we could go. We didn't hold back.

When the day came to head up the mountain, there was a giant film crew, including helicopters, there to shoot the whole thing. We started out quickly and Robby said that when I started to feel fatigued, we could slow down. As we got up the mountain, my adrenaline kicked in. We had never been above the tree line, other than with the simulator, and there was something both beautiful and intense about going eighty miles per hour where all you can see is blue sky. Our Corvette didn't have a roll cage nor were we wearing helmets. If we lost control, it could have been incredibly disastrous, or even deadly for that matter. Robby and I both knew what we signed up for and at the end of the day, we wanted to make our best time possible. That track is intimidating, but we made it to the top in fifteen minutes, which was just six more than the eventual race winner. We weren't registered as official competitors, but our time would have beaten 30 percent of the drivers who competed that day. It was a huge victory for our team and much more challenging than our laps at the Indianapolis Motor Speedway.

When we finished, I was short of breath in the thin Colorado mountain air. As we hit the top, the race promoter came running out. He was going crazy. "Do you know your time? You guys have got to come back and do this again!" As if we'd rehearsed it, Robby and I looked at each other and said, "Nope!" in unison. We did what we came to do, and that was enough. We felt lucky that we finished like we did. When we got to the top, I also found out that about forty-five minutes before we began up the hill, Sheila had *almost* put her foot down to cancel the whole thing. Prior to our run, she and Spencer had ridden up the hill in the BraunAbility van. They were going to greet us at the top and wave the checkered flag. That drive to the top scared her to death, and she knew I was not the type to simply cruise to the top if given the opportunity to go faster. I'm pretty sure that it was Joe who talked her off the ledge. Thank goodness he did because even if she called, I probably would have still competed and blamed it on bad cell service.

Even just a few years prior, I never could have imagined all of these accomplishments. I might be in a chair now, but I still would like to think of myself as an accomplished professional racecar driver, even if it was ages ago. In fact, our Corvette's license plate read: RCR4LIF. Just in case that wasn't clear! It was amazing to see the view at the top of the mountain. It was one of the best payoffs of my life. I was at the top of the world.

* * *

If I thought things couldn't get better—or even more surreal—then I was wrong. Because soon I had an opportunity that I'd dreamed of my entire life. When it comes to racing, there are few names bigger and few people more accomplished than Mario Andretti. The Italian-born driver boasts four IndyCar championships and he's the only driver *EVER* to win an Indy 500, Daytona 500, and a Formula One world championship. I had racing on my mind, so the next time I saw Mario at an IndyCar race I challenged him to race me in matching SAM cars to benefit Conquer Paralysis Now. He agreed immediately, and Arrow built him a car so we could race head-to-head.

The simple idea of this was a thrill for me because I watched Mario win races in the '70s and '80s, and he was one of the legends who inspired me to become a professional racer. Now we were going to share a track—not just any track. We were going to race each other on the road course at the Indianapolis Motor Speedway.

The race marked the first time two semi-autonomous cars raced against each other. For the competition, we both would drive Corvette Stingrays and, like me, Mario would control the car with his head and the sip-and-puff device. Speedway president Doug Boles is always up for a good promotion, but even he thought Mario and I were crazy for this! Mario, who was seventy-seven years old at the time, was always game for a new challenge. Though I'd lost the use of my limbs, I think I was proving that I hadn't lost my need for speed. And the fact that we could use the event to raise money for the foundation was that much better (fans could donate by texting "Sam" or "Mario" to a special number, voting for who they thought would win). The opportunity really spoke to the talent of the Arrow team as much as it did Mario or me. "I've never been so nervous in my life," Mario said before the race. "I haven't had any sleep the last two nights." He really did not want to lose, especially to someone who could not use his limbs!

When the race began, we both revved our engines like two teenagers at a drag race. With the sun shining down, we sped off down the straightaway. We both quickly got over a hundred miles per hour. The road course race was four laps, and we exchanged the lead several times. When I got to the final turn, I could not see him. It turns out that Mario cut the entire corner. He was cheating to beat me! Mario crossed the finish line before me and after the race I jokingly demanded a rematch. I told him that I felt bad he hadn't won at the Speedway in forty-eight years, so I figured he needed the win more than I did. It was all in good fun. Also, for me to cross the finish line for the first time in nearly two decades was monumental. I couldn't help but do donuts after that, tire smoke and all. It was a full-circle moment.

Mario said he was impressed with the car and its responsiveness. There was a bit of a learning curve, too—he couldn't turn his head to check his mirrors like he was used to. He said he had never faced anything like it. Of course, after he won, he said he could sleep again. Mario went on to praise the technology and what it could offer other people. "This is something so positive," he said. "Can you imagine how many lives this will affect?" Sharing the track with Mario reminded me why we keep pushing forward: Because there really is no finish line with what can be accomplished.

Not only did Arrow stand by the technology, but they also didn't patent it. They wanted it to be available for free to anyone if they could use it to help others. That kind of servant mentality in corporate America is rare, especially in larger or publicly traded companies. Next, we started to think about adding artificial intelligence to the car to help with speed, handling, and safety—the possibilities were limitless. From the start, we knew this project was about more than a car—it was about giving people back their independence. There are around six million people just in America living with some form of paralysis and if this technology could help even a fraction of them, it would be worth it. For me, it was a level of independence I never thought I would have again. It was not going to help me walk my daughter down the aisle—at least not yet—but being able to drive myself again was its own kind of miracle.

Luckily for me, there was still more driving to be done. This time it wasn't on a track or up a treacherous mountain. Instead, it was on real-life city streets. For nearly two decades, I'd only been out in the streets in a cab or vans—always driven around by another person. Since I earned a driver's license in Nevada, I could now drive myself around *anywhere.* One of the places we went for me to drive was

Times Square in New York City. Harry Smith from the *Today* show tagged along. I even popped the top off on the car so people could see me and admire the SAM car. The best part of it was that they couldn't even tell I was paralyzed, I just looked like your everyday guy driving a Corvette . . . unless, of course, they realized I was not using my hands!

On another occasion, we took the car out to the streets of Boston. I went with some of the Arrow engineers to MIT to speak about our technology and the SAM car. Joe also rented time on a racetrack in western Massachusetts, and a student racing team came out to drive and experiment with our car. Then, Joe, who is always trying to think of the next way we can make a headline, had the bright idea to drive the SAM car on the Freedom Trail, the 2.5-mile stretch in the city that connects sixteen significant historical sights. Joe, who is originally from the area, wanted to shoot a commercial there for a promo video. It would combine the latest tech with the oldest landmarks in the country.

It turned out to be more difficult than we thought it would be. The weather was bad and there was a lot of traffic. We were going down these tiny Boston streets, and I was following a member of our crew. They turned down a pedestrian mall. Joe was in the car behind me, and he remembers screaming from his car, "You can't go there, you can't go there!" Of course nobody heard Joe. Well . . . then we drove by a Boston cop. This was only a short while after the horrific Boston Marathon bombing and so the area was often filled with police. The police officer flipped on his lights, and he pulled me over. At first, I wasn't sure if Joe was staging another fake pull over like he'd done in Vegas. No—this one was for real.

Joe and Mike Long had joked about this happening. What made it worse was that I stupidly didn't have my license on me and our registration was back in the van. When the cop came up to my window, he said, "License and registration."

But I could only reply, "Sir, I can't show them to you."

"Are you driving this car?" he asked.

"Yes," I said.

The officer just looked at me quizzically. We were there for more than thirty minutes as he tried to understand just what the heck was going on. Joe came up to explain. Using his native Boston accent, he tried to get chummy with the officer. Eventually, the cop agreed to let us drive away, but only straight to where my van was parked. He said, "You go there, get in the van, and I don't want to see you again." We happily agreed. As it was all going down, Joe said he texted Mike Long, who replied, "No bail for any of you!" And he meant it. Thankfully we didn't need it. And thank goodness, my license still hasn't been revoked!

That mishap didn't deter me from continuing to drive the car out in the real world. One more box I needed to check was taking my wife out on a date. When you're a teenager, all you can think about is taking a girl out in your new ride. Well, if you're paralyzed and you haven't driven in over a decade, that feeling comes back. So, in 2017, the same year the Nevada Sports Hall of Fame inducted me into their ranks, I wanted to take Sheila out on the town. While in the Bay area for an IndyCar race, I picked her up and we drove across San Francisco's Golden Gate Bridge. After that, we went on a dinner date and felt young and in love again. I'll always remember that moment.

We kept pushing the envelope. As Savannah says, "If you take racing out of Dad, it's just not Dad anymore." Over the years, we went back to the Indy 500 several times to show off the car and to go *faster*. In 2016, I drove 154 miles per hour on the track. Later, I went 192 miles per hour at Nellis Air Force Base while racing a jet. Yes, you read that correctly. Eventually we hit speeds of 213 miles per hour at the Kennedy Space Center in the shadows of the space shuttle. In 2015, I drove my kids around the streets of Washington, DC, to commemorate the twenty-fifth anniversary of the signing of the Americans with Disabilities Act. We took the SAM car to England in 2021 and 2022 to show off what we'd done internationally at the Goodwood Hill Climb. The BBC ran so many stories on us it generated over five *billion* impressions. We drove the car in the legendary Hong Kong Technology Park to great success. Back in the States, we were featured on Jay Leno's television show, *Jay Leno's Garage*. All of this gave our work credibility on a global stage and more than anything it gave me reasons to get out of bed each morning. My work with Arrow allowed me to feel normal again.

16

YOU WANT TO DO WHAT?

WE HAVE PRECIOUS FEW baby pictures of our son, Spencer. It's one of the things I regret about my accident. He was only six months old when it happened. Today, Spencer is in his mid-twenties, and he recently began his own racing career. *Gulp.* Yup, you read that correctly. As I watch him, in the back of my mind, I can't help but think: *It* can't happen a third time, can it?

Spencer hadn't yet graduated from college when he first talked to me about racing—he jokingly calls it his "pandemic quarter-life crisis." We were at our home in Las Vegas, and he was helping me with something on the computer. He slyly typed in the name of three racing schools. "Hey, do you know anybody at any of these?" he asked. I said, "What for . . . ?" And he said he wanted to enroll. We talked about it a little, but I told him that was a conversation he needed to have with his mother. I honestly thought she would shoot it down immediately. I was going to let her be the bad guy.

Months later in the spring of 2022, he came to us again and said, "I don't want any regrets in ten years. No rock unturned. I just really need to give this a try." He talked to us glowingly about going to Indianapolis with me every May since he was a kid to see the Indy 500. He talked about how much the sport and its culture has meant to him over the decades. Somehow, he got Sheila on board and then I had no choice but to agree. It would have been hypocritical of me to say no.

He enrolled in the Skip Barber Racing School, which had a three-day course in Austin, Texas, to learn the basics, from downshifting to braking and various exercises. After that, I put him through a rigorous six-month course. If he wanted to become a professional, I wanted to show him what that really meant. To begin his training, I put him in an old truck—if it broke, he had to fix it—and told him to drive to Indianapolis from Vegas to race all summer. The go-kart he would drive when he got to Indy came in a crate and he had to build it piece by piece. I connected him with people there who could help and support him, but he had to do it all himself. He took classes, he studied the proper nutrition necessary for top athletes. I had to make it difficult for him, which meant me not being there. I remember the first time I told my dad that I wanted to race. He said, "I'll be at the races, but you've got to figure the rest out!" Tough love sometimes is the only way.

His first race was at Whiteland Raceway Park, south of Indianapolis. Sheila and I were there to watch him compete. At twenty-two years old, he started in twenty-fifth place and fought for every inch. He finished twentieth. He worked his way past several drivers, and I could feel my jaw clenching as I watched it all unfold from my wheelchair.

He continued racing regularly at Whiteland, and, in every race, kids much younger beat him. They had been racing much longer. Imagine applying for a job out of college and you don't get it because there are kids ten years younger with ten years more experience. That was the feeling he had for every race he ran. It was a summer that taught him how to lose. His "Summer of Humility."

We had never seen him chase something like that or *want* something so badly. That was encouraging. When he came home from those first races, he looked dejected but somehow undeterred. He'd get back in his car the next day, beat his head against the steering wheel a handful of times, and then know what he had to do for the next one. He showed initiative like never before. He was on the phone asking older racing veterans for advice, and he began fundraising for his future . . . Cold calling, asking for sponsorships.

Of course, I thought he could be doing more. And I'm sure he thought I could be helping more. Sheila heard it all from both sides. She would just tell us to talk to each other instead of her. But over time, racing has brought Spencer and me closer. We talk and spend more time together than ever. It is our silver lining.

As a boy, he wasn't exactly the most driven or athletic kid. In high school, he showed promise in theater as an actor, but that didn't inspire him enough to continue it later in college. At my alma mater, Pepperdine University, he earned a degree in Fine Arts. He's a very gifted painter and sculptor—imaginative, and talented at just about anything creative he tries—but none of those pursuits seemed to stick for long.

Spencer didn't even want to attend college initially, but Sheila and I strongly encouraged him to try it, especially since he had no alternative plans. After graduation, when he told his mother that he wanted to race cars, she was vehemently against it. For her, it was fear mixed with heartbreak. She had already lived through the unthinkable when my accident happened, and she's been by my side ever since: through every hospital stay, every surgery, every sleepless night, every morning spent lifting me out of bed and helping me face another day. She's done all that not out of obligation, but out of love. It's not hard to understand her wanting anything *but* a life in racing for her only son. When he announced his plan Sheila questioned why he would want to start at his age.

Most drivers at elite levels begin racing at around five years old; some do so even earlier, before preschool. They sign professional contracts at twelve or thirteen. We put Spencer and his sister, Savannah, in go-karts when they were just becoming teenagers.

It was something of a test. Knowing that they had racing in their blood, Sheila and I wanted to see if either would take to it, if it would spark anything in them. If either would wake us up at the crack of dawn demanding that we take them to the track to practice again. Of the two, I thought Savannah was the most likely. She's like me—determined, strong-willed, hardheaded, and competitive. Even today, Spencer says he could benefit from having some of her fire. But neither child really pushed for it and so Sheila and I let it go. *Thank God we dodged that bullet* . . . or so we thought! But lately it's all Spencer can talk about.

The key for any racer is to not think about what could happen if things go wrong. He says he doesn't. I said the same. My father did, too. Of course there is always a voice somewhere in our minds suggesting it. It's a catch-22, as Spencer says; you can't think about it and you can't think about *not* thinking about it, either. Because then you're *thinking* about it.

It's a grind. To keep his mind sharp, he drives regularly on the simulator and works with a sports psychologist, the same one I worked with when I was driving. Ronn Langford is an eighty-five-year-old expert in the field. (Yes, you read his age correctly!). He is a laid-back Colorado guy who can work wonders with the mind. Ronn is big on training athletes to think like a computer, to process, program, and reprogram based on a given situation. Whenever something bad happens to Spencer on the track—if he loses a race, if something breaks on his car, if he can't go as fast as he wants, if he crashes—Ronn tells him to imagine the issue afterward like a big hot-air balloon, then to put the memory or the problem in the basket and watch it float away, getting smaller and smaller on the horizon. When his mind is clear, he can go back to the track and see how his brain has responded to the exercise. With racing, a tenth of a second around a track can be the difference between winning and losing. At the highest level, drivers are traveling a football field per second in their million-dollar cars. That's what Spencer is working toward—to clear his mind, control his thoughts, and find that tiny edge where races are won.

* * *

The first time Sheila and I saw Spencer crash was at Michelin Raceway Road Atlanta (also known as "Road Atlanta") in 2023. He hit a barrier and bent his right rear suspension. Thankfully, he had enough runoff that he didn't smack the wall *too hard*. He lost control making a turn at 115 miles per hour in a car that could go 125 miles per hour. He thinks he hit the wall at about 50 miles per hour. When I asked him what happened he said he wasn't going fast enough, so he started *trying* to go faster, even though the balance of the car was not where it needed to be. This is the worst thing a driver can do. You can't force speed simply by pushing harder. It has to be natural. It's all about the feel, technique, and experience—things you can only learn over time, organically.

Crashing, and doing so in front of us, threw him off mentally for a while. More hot-air balloons were in his future to remedy all that. He had to get past it. Ronn wants him to learn tai chi next to help with relaxation and balance. Spencer can look at data and video, and he can work in the most precise simulators, but if he's unable to get his mind into a regular, steady, and consistent flow state, he won't be able to succeed on the track. According to Spencer, the only two times in his life when he felt that feeling of being in a "flow state" was making art and racing. He says he can paint when he is sixty. Racing is now or never.

Realistically, Spencer has only a few years to learn everything he needs to know if he wants to catch up to his peers. Think about it this way: Would the Green Bay Packers draft a hotshot twenty-two-year-old quarterback out of college or a twenty-seven-year-old who picked up the game late in life? This only adds pressure to Spencer's routine. Also, racing is not cheap. Each day on the track, thousands of dollars go out the window. It's the most competitive sport when it comes to trying to secure funding for an individual team or driver. There are two ways to make money in racing. Either you get so good that you earn a salary, or you work so hard that you find your own long-term funding. Costs can escalate into the millions in higher levels of racing. It's not easy—although nothing worthwhile ever is.

As I've said, my father started me racing when I was five years old. But I was in my early thirties the first time I got in an IndyCar, a fact Spencer reminded me and his mother of many times when he was working to convince us of this dream. And what were we supposed to say? No parent wants to snuff out their child's hopes. In fact, all you ever dream of is that they can find their passion and excel at it. But when I got back into racing after college, I won races and awards right off the bat. I couldn't be stopped (until, of course, I was). It was a different time then; I can admit that. The cars were much less technical, and racing budgets were considerably smaller.

The great news is that Spencer has improved each season. In 2023, he raced in the Skip Barber F4 series, managing a couple of podiums and fifth in the points championship. In 2024, the Radical Cup North America series seemed like a good step up in performance (lap times average ten sec/lap faster than the F4 car) with very large fields of drivers who had similar experience levels. That year, in a summer Radical Cup race in Toronto, Spencer qualified second, which was his best effort all season. In a race in Wisconsin a few weeks prior, he finished third. Ultimately, he finished fourth in the Championship of the Pro 1500 series.

He felt like regular podiums were attainable, but he needed to know what it feels like to lead races and win. Unless you are winning regularly, it is very difficult to find outside funding. He decided to stay in Radical Cup for another season to see if he could win, not just contend. By the end of 2025, he had finished second on several occasions and even finished the season second in the overall championship. A huge accomplishment. Spencer had the pace to win races. As of this writing, he is still only twenty-six and clearly has the desire. I wonder how far he will go. I don't mean to say we have our hopes up for any storybook ending, but we're not ruling it out, either.

* * *

Growing up, Spencer used to ask us questions about his childhood. All kids do. They want to know what they were like as babies or as five-year-olds on their first day of kindergarten. But early on, we missed a lot of that time. It's my fault. My family didn't ask to be part of IndyCar. It wasn't their dream to be in racing; it was mine. Since it was my choice, I can live with the results of my accident. The harder part, though, is seeing them have to live with it and the impact it's had on their lives. Spencer will ask us, "When did I first walk?" or "What was my first word?" And we honestly don't have a precise answer for him. We were so consumed with my recovery and trying to survive those first couple years. Thank goodness he and his sister grew up to be remarkable human beings. They are compassionate, empathetic, and bright. They're the best proof I could ever have that love can outlast tragedy.

For a long time, though, he and I didn't connect. I've always been driven by competition and sports, but he has always been driven by the arts and other interests. When I was young, I didn't always connect with my father, either—except when one of us was racing. Racing gave us more than enough to talk about. After Dad's accident, when he couldn't race anymore, we drifted apart. When I started racing, we connected more. Sheila will say that all she cares about is that we always stay close as a family, and that Spencer and Savannah are good versions of themselves. It's hard to imagine who they would've become if I'd never gotten hurt. Living alongside someone in a wheelchair—and seeing how the world reacts—has given them a kind of empathy and awareness that can't be taught. They've seen both the kindness and the ignorance people can show, and it's shaped who they are.

I have wondered if Spencer really wanted to race or if he was somehow doing it to connect with me or even to make up for what racing had taken from me and his grandfather. Maybe if he could conquer the sport, he would be doing it for the other men in his family? It wasn't as if he could be anonymous out there. I tend to stick out in my chair and racers know me or at least know my story. So, even on a small track in Whiteland, Spencer can feel the eyeballs fixed on him. People watch, wondering how he will carry on the Schmidt name. Spencer described it this way:

> *It's weird how you can tune things out. I could see people across the track point and whisper. But I was like, "Okay, if I can't handle this, I'm not going to be able to handle the rest of my*

life." That was a good introduction to the fact that I've got to make a name for myself if I'm going to succeed. Clearly there are two big shoes to fill. But I have to make my own pair.

When people ask Spencer why racing means so much more to him now as an adult, he says it wasn't up to him as a kid. The same reason why we don't have many baby pictures or even memories of his first few years is the same reason why we never put him in a go-kart at four or five years old. He says he appreciates being given the space to make his own choices. Still, some part of him wishes we had pushed him more toward driving.

Not only were Sheila and I occupied with my survival in Spencer's early years, but we wanted *him* to decide what he wanted to do. It was the last thing on Sheila's mind to put him in a car that could go over a hundred miles per hour before he even turned ten. Spencer was a shy and a rather indecisive kid growing up. Most of the things he did as a boy were the result of what his friends wanted to do. That wasn't racing. The truth is, though, he's been around racing his whole life. And when I started to take a step back from the business side of things with my IndyCar team a few years ago, he realized how much the racing world meant to him. As I started to phase out, he decided to start *phasing in*. He didn't want to lose his ties to it and that sparked something new in him.

I had always worked to build my racing teams into something that felt like a family and Spencer has responded to that. It wasn't just me; the racing industry truly is a family. The Indy Racing League had a community center and ministry at most of the races for the families of drivers, owners, and other personnel. It was a big part of their life.

Spencer admits he has questioned if he is doing this for *him* or for *us*, if he is doing this because his last name is Schmidt? Or maybe it is for some sense of glamour? I think the only answer to those questions right now is that he just loves everything about it. It's intoxicating. To know every inch of a car and every inch of a track, to compete against the best in the world, the rush of speed. It's one of those sports that you can fall deeper into with time.

Some people talk about *having it* on their first day behind the wheel of a racecar—the *I'm-never-going-back* feeling. But Spencer didn't. Instead, he started to look at it with an artist's eye. For him, the sport is not about the rush of adrenaline. He's not a junkie for that side of it. He's more of a flow state kind of guy. He has been known to say, "Perfect driving is just being in perfect communication with the car." He is right, you do have to be one with the car when you go those speeds—150, 200, 225 miles per hour. It has to be in your subconscious. No lapses. I can tell from the sidelines, with every inch of progress, he loves it more.

Back when Dad or I was coming up, the sport was different. There wasn't nearly as much infrastructure built around it, which has its pros and cons today. Spencer is trying to drink from a fire hose; there is so much information coming at him. The benefit this current generation has today, though, is technology. They can use simulators. You don't have to train every moment out there on the track, which helps to save money and time. That's one of the new safety measures that exists today. Simulators act as practice runs. After all, my accident came during a practice session—even those can be life-threatening. Spencer can make a lot of his mistakes in front of a screen. That training is paying off. In every series we put him in, he goes from the back of the pack at the start of the year, to fighting for wins at the end of it. He keeps improving his physical condition, too. Today, he's in the best shape of his life.

As time passes, Spencer gives us more and more reasons to believe he has a driving career ahead of him. I've raced at the highest level, but nothing compares to the feeling of watching him chase his dream. When he drives, I feel every heartbeat, every turn, like I was behind the wheel myself. I've never been more proud of him—and more nervous.

I've seen so much of what racing can mean to someone's life, both good and bad. Maybe you're a four-time Indy 500 winner or maybe you own a team or maybe you just feel at home in the garages, pits, or in a support role. Thankfully, I know that no matter what happens in his life, Spencer will continue to have a spot in the racing world if he wants one. If it's more behind the scenes than behind the wheel, that would put his mother at ease. Ultimately, he has to decide his own future and be willing to put in the hard work to achieve it.

17

DRIVEN

AT COSTUME PARTIES, I like to keep things interesting. When I show up dressed as a crash test dummy, mask and all, people don't quite know what to say. Sheila is by my side in a lab coat—complete with clipboard, pocket protector, and studious glasses—we think it is hilarious. It's not the costume that throws people; it's the fact that I'm in my wheelchair. I just can't help it. You've got to keep a sense of humor about yourself in hard times. If I wasn't laughing at the situation, I'd probably be crying. People don't always know how to act around someone in a wheelchair, so I try to make it easy on them. If I can make them laugh, then I feel like I have won.

It's not easy, though. Nothing about my life has been easy these past twenty-six years, least of all giving up the control I once knew well. I thought I learned the meaning of perseverance when I was ten years old watching my dad rehab from his accident. Or the effort it took to build a successful business or become a professional racecar driver. That was just an introduction. I didn't truly learn perseverance until I faced my own paralysis. Here I am twenty-six years later, still in a wheelchair and still pushing forward, and doing everything I can to help others like me—occasionally, that means dressing up like a crash test dummy on Halloween to remind myself, and everyone else, that it's okay to laugh!

When I think about what happened to me, I have to give thanks for what didn't happen. I didn't incur a brain injury, and I am not on a ventilator. My spinal cord injury could have been higher up on my neck and threatened my life even more. I am grateful for all that I have been able to do, which I believe is much more than I would have had I not been injured. It might be cliche to say, but I believe that everything happens for a reason and that God has a plan for each of us. I may not be able to put my arms around my kids, but I have forged a life that has so much meaning, connection and joy.

Now, instead of thinking about getting around a track faster than the next guy, I am asking questions like, "How can we solve the problem of paralysis in a shorter amount of time than we first thought possible?" And as I continue to strive toward that, the journey has led me to create what may be the proudest achievement of my life: *DRIVEN by Sam Schmidt.*

Before I tell you more about that, let me tell you the story of my friend, the insanely talented driver Robert Wickens. As I've said before, the racing community is tight-knit. We want to beat each other on race day, but if something tragic happens, we all rally. That is exactly what we did in 2018.

Robert Wickens joined our race team and earned the pole in his first race with us, the Firestone Grand Prix of St. Petersburg. Three quarters of the way through his rookie season, Robert suffered a horrific accident at the ABC Supply 500 at Pocono Raceway. He made an aggressive move on the opening lap and by the time he realized it, he had lost control at two-hundred-plus miles per hour and was launched into the catch fence, which is always unforgiving. For a few terrifying moments, we all thought we had lost him. Everyone was holding their breath.

After first responders pulled him out, he was immediately put in a helicopter and taken to the closest hospital. A couple of hours later, we learned that his spinal cord was bruised, and his hands, feet, and legs were badly injured. Thankfully, there was no brain damage. His fiancée was out of town at the time, but the community flew her in to see him immediately. His parents and brother were in Toronto, so they drove down as well in constant communication with the team. Every team has a comprehensive playbook for situations like this. We all hope to never to have to use it.

After a long series of surgeries and treatment, which took place in Pennsylvania and Indianapolis, Robert was considered a paraplegic and was told he would never walk again. It was the fall of 2018, and he was just twenty-nine years old. If there's one thing I've learned in life, it's that determination and hope can rewrite expectations. Robert's first goal wasn't to race again—it was to stand and dance with Karli at their wedding. And just one year after the accident, he did exactly that. By 2022, thanks to intensive rehabilitation and his amazing resilience, he made an incredible comeback. He even raced full-time again, beginning with the Michelin Pilot Challenge, driving a car with adapted hand controls. His return was the result of relentless hard work and courage, but also the progress made possible by years of research from our foundation and others around the country committed to changing the future of rehabilitation. Having this information and technology at his disposal gave Robert an advantage that racers like me never had. A few decades earlier, his story might have turned out very differently. Today, he's thriving—married to Karli, father to Wesley, Dash, and Daisy—and once again living his dream behind the wheel.

What if you aren't someone like Robert or me with professional athlete insurance? What if you simply can't find good care? I've encountered countless lifetime healthcare executives who just don't care as much about patients as they do the bottom line. That's where my dream of DRIVEN was born. If you get injured like Robert or I did, life can quickly feel like an avalanche of hardship. The financial stress is insane. The pressure on your family is intense. Even the most intimate parts of life—your marriage, your sense of self—are tested in ways you can't imagine. Counseling often becomes necessary but is increasingly not covered by insurance. I've met thousands of people in wheelchairs since my accident, and I know what they're going through. Through it all, I know how lucky I am to have Sheila. She says today, "I would take Sam like this over not having him any day of the week." Truly, I don't know if I could have survived all I've put her through, if the roles were reversed.

That's the thing. When you're paralyzed, you need so much from others. From nurses like Anna to physical therapists to specialized transportation to assistants like Myra, who for twenty-six-plus years has continued to indulge my crazy ideas. One time, she even got me in a wet suit to go scuba diving, which was like, as she puts it, "Putting toothpaste back into the tube." You also need your family. You can achieve anything you want in your recovery, but you have to be willing to put the work in and integrate others into your life. That's what I tell people all over the world. There is always a reason to stop or give up. When Robert got hurt, I thought we were cursed as a team. But even then, I knew we had to push through and persevere, if for no other reason than to make sure he got back on his feet, *literally.*

It is also important to maintain a positive attitude. In my case, I try to make jokes as often as I can. Like when TSA agents search me at the airport and ask if I have any sensitive areas to the touch. "No," I respond. "But I wish I did!" I also have the racecar that I was driving at the time of the crash in Orlando. Most people might want to bury that memory and move on, but not me. I restored it. It sits in my garage at home in Las Vegas, in what Sheila calls my "I love me" room. To me, it's not a symbol of loss—it's a reminder of survival. I don't steer clear of it, I embrace it. I'm proud of what I've done since my accident. That car keeps me humble and reminds me of how far my life has come.

I've visited many hospitals over the past few decades and had more than a few tough conversations with newly injured patients and their families. I don't sugarcoat it. I say to patients, "It sucks. There is no way around it. Your life has changed in a major way, but now you have a choice: Do you want to go home and let your body wilt away or do you want to make something of your life? Do you want to turn tragedy into an opportunity?" People don't always want to hear that, not when the future still feels so difficult. Both patients and family often prefer coddling in their hour of need. Time in rehabilitation is increasingly limited, so you need to maximize every opportunity to gain independence. That's how Pat Rummerfield treated me after my accident, and I will forever be grateful. Once you accept your reality, you can make your move forward. You can't always control what happens to you, but you can control what happens next.

That is the heart of DRIVEN—a place for those who want to push ahead but don't have the resources to do it properly. Not everyone can be part of a family business that does well or win a game show for a head start. Given the option, I wouldn't be in this chair either. But because I am, I'm able to help and inspire others. And thankfully, my children have followed suit. I've always hoped Savannah would take over my business and every day, even with a growing family, she's stepped up. She helps run our Day at the Races programs and fundraisers and is intimately involved in all aspects of our foundation. And Spencer, too, has shown more interest in the nitty-gritty behind-the-scenes work of our efforts. I believe the

Schmidt family name and the purpose behind it will continue long after my dad and I are gone.

When our first DRIVEN facility in Las Vegas opened in 2018, just months after Robert's accident, we realized the possibility of our mission. We made intensive rehabilitation, care, and community available to those who needed it. The facility is 7,500 square feet of hope. As we were building it, we had no idea the impact it would fuel in Las Vegas. Now we do and we're ready for more. We've raised millions of dollars to make this pilot location thrive and to bring another mega-center to Indianapolis. And we're not stopping there. We've only just begun.

For the first fifteen years of my recovery, I only had one definition of what a cure would mean to me: walking again, or at least embracing Sheila and my kids with my own two arms. Now, though, after seeing so many goals achieved by others along the way, that definition has expanded a hundred-fold. Today, I realize that a "cure" might mean getting a driver's license, helping someone stand again, or inspiring someone to simply get out of bed in the morning. I could never have understood this when I was a young racer. My entire focus was on reaching the finish line before anyone else. Now I know there is no finish line. Each year, there are thousands and thousands of new spinal cord injuries. And if you include strokes, brain injuries, and other neurological disorders, which require the same type of recovery programs, that number increases into the millions. The number of people helping those who are injured or suffering is small. It's *now* my life's work to change that.

I'm not trying to hide my injuries. I'm trying to defy them, and the odds that come with them. So many people have helped me along the way, and I want to turn around and do the same for others. That's why I don't feel ashamed when my kids and I go into a car dealership and no one comes to help us, or when people look at me in a restaurant as my wife or kids feed me, or when I'm on a plane and I can't control myself from tipping over during turbulence. Even when my four-hundred-pound wheelchair almost sinks a pontoon boat because I'm too stubborn to stay on shore. I just laugh. These are the moments that remind me I'm living, not surviving.

I consider myself an example of improvement, not a statistic of loss. Over the years, I have been humbled to receive several awards: the Gateway to a Cure Award; New Ability Award; Visionary Leadership Award from the Christopher & Dana Reeve Paralysis Foundation; the Distinguished Alumni Award from Pepperdine University; the Humanitarian Award from the Las Vegas Walk of Stars Foundation; and the 2013 Courage Award. I've also served on the board of directors for Desert Canyon Rehabilitation Center and Speedway Children's Charities. I'm very proud of all that but by no means am I finished. I did not list these awards to brag, but rather to emphasize that there is life after tragedy. It will never be easy, but it can be extraordinary.

I turned sixty years old in August 2024, while working on the first draft of this book. I wouldn't say my physical state is getting *better.* I'm doing fine but Father Time remains undefeated, and I know that. Still, there was a time when no one thought I would turn forty. I beat those odds by more than two decades, but I know how precious my time is these days.

So, in 2024, I chose to step away from racing to focus on the goals that are most important to me today. I had already scaled back some in 2021 when McLaren Racing bought a 75 percent stake in the team. At that time, we rebranded to Arrow McLaren SP and McLaren CEO, Zak Brown, was installed as the chairman. Ric Peterson and I shared the remaining 25 percent until the end of 2024. That's when we made the decision to sell the rest to McLaren, an iconic legendary brand with a rich history in global motorsports. The team is now known as Arrow McLaren IndyCar Team. It was bittersweet, but my heart will always be with the team that we built from the hospital room up. They are in excellent hands, which meant it was time for me to shift my focus to my dream of opening more DRIVEN facilities around the country. As I said, "*Racing is my passion, DRIVEN is my purpose.*"

* * *

If you're lucky, you are always learning new lessons in life. And as you do, you can humbly apply your wisdom to new endeavors. That's exactly what I did in the mid-2020s with our newest DRIVEN facility. While we had our first operation in Las Vegas, it became clear we needed more capacity. We knew we wanted to keep the facility in Nevada, my full-time residence, but we decided to open a new, bigger, and even better building in Indianapolis. It is a 114,000-square-foot facility on ten acres of land. It's monstrous in the best of ways and seeks to be a one-stop location for people who are facing a neurological condition.

After a long search, we decided on the former Five Seasons Family Sports Club on the north side of the city. When we found it, we knew it would be our training facility, our rehabilitation center, and our research hub. We wanted to have enough space to collaborate with other organizations that serve the community, and to partner with local healthcare professionals to offer care to those who needed it. It brought me great joy to see the new facility open in the fall of 2024. The mayor of Carmel and Indiana Governor Eric Holcomb's chief of staff were among the many who attended to wish us well and tour the space. The center includes an adaptive sports arena, aquatic therapy pools, a functional garden, a pediatric center, a training kitchen and apartment, meeting rooms, and much more. Simply put, there is nothing else like it in the United States, possibly the world.

DRIVEN is the most important work of my life. It's more than a legacy, it's a bridge to a better future. Today, I no longer wonder what I might have done on the racetrack. What I've seen DRIVEN accomplish through the hope it can offer people means far more. I'm proud that my story has helped make improvements to cars, tracks, and safety equipment. More than that, I'm proud that I know that my life is no longer just about me. And I'm not going to waste any more time thinking that it is.

Prior to 2020, I couldn't say no to anything—ironically, I just couldn't sit still. I was trying to fill up every empty jar that came my way. The COVID-19 pandemic changed me forever. I stopped traveling. I had to heal after getting sick with the illness, I think, before anyone even knew what COVID was. Then, my daughter was married, and I was able to dance with her in a dream come true moment. Then I took the exoskeleton suit to a race and surprised my team members. I even shocked one of the EMT first responders who pulled me from the wreckage in Orlando some twenty-one years earlier. I found out he was at the same race as I was. So I found him. I stood up behind him, someone tapped him on the shoulder, and he damn near fainted! We both had a moment, then shed a tear together.

My goal is to continue to pay it forward. I've never wanted to be a soapbox guy. Instead, I've always just wanted to lead by example. Now that we've opened our latest DRIVEN center and have our headquarters stationed in Indy, we want to create satellite programs all over the country. I believe we can do it. We want to be the place people can turn when they feel like they don't have any other place to go. Today, I have four important things in my life. My relationship with God, my family, my share in Dan Wheldon's Indianapolis 500 win in 2011, and DRIVEN. That's the list. And it fills me with joy and pride every day. It may have taken sixty years, but I can see that I've evolved from a man focused entirely on himself to one entirely focused on wanting others to win. Today, I care about the millions of individuals who are living like me in the world. And if I can help them, I will.

The most tragic thing in my life would have been to think that my accident was the most tragic thing in my life. No. Instead, it made me who I am today. There are countless examples of people who are in crisis. A car crash, an accident, a slip and fall, a stroke, a soldier injured in combat—any one of these events can turn a family upside down. I believe that we can do even more for those who need it. In fact, I'm sure of it. That's why I get up every morning.

18

NO FINISH LINE

EVERY YEAR, our family sends out Christmas cards. One year we included a Bible verse that's come to define so much of my life: James 1:12 reads, "Blessed is the man who perseveres under trial because when he has stood the test, he will receive the crown of life that God has promised to those who love him."

I'll tell you a secret: When I'm asleep in bed, and I'm dreaming, I'm never in my wheelchair. I am always walking. My dream life has never changed, and in some ways that's a reminder of the promise of Heaven and the promise that I *will* walk again. Faith is such a crucial part of my life. I lean on it. I leaned on it long before that hospital room in Orlando, and it's held me up ever since.

I know a thing or two about chasing dreams, about losing them, and about finding new ones. It can be a battle to keep your head above water. When I was younger, all I cared about was going fast. *Faster, always faster.* I craved control, and not just when it came to my racecar, but I wanted my fingerprints on everything. If it had my name on it, it was going to be perfect. That level of control and perfection is impossible when you're in my chair. Small tasks like bathing and brushing my teeth must be delegated, and they take longer. Patience is not something I was generally known for, but now I *have* to have it. As a result, my life and my approach to it has changed. For the better, I'm certain. I've been ten times more successful and productive than I would have been if I hadn't been injured. And I owe it all to the people who've let me in their lives. When you hear about those who've done well in business or other fields, the easiest thing to think about is them on their own burning the midnight oil. But that's just not how it works. We all depend on others. I know I do.

As I reflect on the past twenty-six years of my life, everything my family, my race team, and our foundation have been able to accomplish, I'm extremely proud and grateful. I could never have done it without the mentors and friends in my life, like Willis Johnson, Forrest Lucas, Ralph Braun, Mike Long, and my father, among many others. Their belief in me gave me a reason to keep pushing forward, even when life felt impossible.

My life looks nothing like I thought it would, but it is much fuller than I expected after the accident and reality set in. My community is larger. I have spent much more time with my family. I've learned to delegate and lean on other people, and in doing so, I've accomplished so much more than I ever could have alone. People sometimes ask if I think everything happened for a reason, if this was somehow meant to be, and I can honestly say *yes*. God gave me this life, and though I often wrestle with it, I believe He knew what He was doing. It's made me stronger. It's made the people around me stronger. And I hope, in some small way, it's made the world a better place.

The truth is, no one has much control over what happens next—I learned that a long time ago. What we *can* control is how we respond. That's why, even now, I refuse to slow down. I haven't sat on a beach and read a book in nearly three decades. Instead, I've bumped into more tables, chairs, and furniture over the past twenty-six years than I care to admit. I have even taken recently to wearing shin guards to protect my legs from running into my desk. As you get older and lose the ability to do certain things, the only way to persevere is to replace what you lose with something better. This applies to *anyone*. I don't mind the difficulty. I'd rather stay sharp, stay positive, and keep moving forward—if not for myself, then for my family.

Thankfully, my children have learned the power of positivity as well. Spencer says there were times in his life when he was angry at God and wondering why this was his experience. But he says he has learned to catch himself when he is having a bad day, "Ultimately, I have no excuse." Hearing that kind of perspective from my son fills me with pride, reminding me that, despite everything we've been through, they learned gratitude, grit, and how to live with hope. Savannah shares that same outlook:

> *The world doesn't revolve around us. The world tells us that happiness comes from success or having nice things, but watching how my parents rebuilt after the accident changed everything for me. I've learned that joy comes from showing up for people, being present, and living with as much purpose as possible. And that's the legacy I will teach my kids, too!*

There have been a few times in my life when I truly thought I would die. It started in those early days following my accident, when my life hung in the balance. There was the time I was on that terrifying flight with Jeff and my oxygen tube popped off. I couldn't reach for it, couldn't signal for help. I just lay there gasping, praying someone would notice. Another time, I was flat on my back being rolled into a CAT scan, and the same thing happened. I was blinking wildly hoping to signal for help, but I was inside the machine. Nobody was there. Nobody knew. My vision blurred, and I thought I saw the light before someone finally returned to the room and fixed it. There was also a day that little Savannah tried to feed me a piece of cantaloupe, and I accidentally got it lodged in my throat. She was terrified, thinking she'd killed her dad. The fire department showed up, and I was rushed to the hospital. It is in those moments when your life flashes before your eyes, where everything becomes clear.

That clarity, for me, is the importance of my family. My kids and, now, my grandkids are the most important things in my world. Yes! I am a proud, proud Opa now. Savannah and Adam blessed us with two lovely grandchildren, London Mae and Callum Samuel. The moment I met London, my first grandchild, suddenly nothing else mattered nearly as much. My priorities were refocused. Other than my family and DRIVEN, most other things took a back seat.

When my kids were young, they wanted nothing more than to be picked up by their dad, and I wanted nothing more than to pick them up. There were lots of things I couldn't do, but I had to focus on things I could do. I needed to be present with my family and to make life feel somewhat normal. As they got older, each year I tried to do something with them that was unique and out of the norm for someone in my situation. I never had a bucket list, per se. Whether or not to create one has always been a question for me. Many people create bucket lists as a way to set goals, to have something to shoot for. My entire *life* has been my bucket list. I worked to achieve my ultimate goal in life every day—to compete in the Indy 500. Of course there were also daily goals, but I'm not the type of person who needs to make a formal list. If I want to do something, I do the research, set it up, and make it happen. Even prior to my accident I understood that life is short!

Every year I have been inspired by new adventures. One year, I found a way to scuba dive, and it was one of my all-time favorite things to do. I had received my open water certification way back at Pepperdine as an elective course. Fast-forward decades later and I ended up at the Tampa Aquarium, which offers an accessible program where they put you in a wet suit, gear you up, and provide you with two buddies underwater. It took a lot of work. The tank had over 2,000 varieties of fish! One, a bright silver fish about the size of my mask, kept seeing its reflection in my mask and poking at it repeatedly. Of course, I couldn't move it away. Honestly, I didn't want to. I felt *normal* there under the water, my limbs floating. Doesn't sound like much, but it felt like a breakthrough at the time.

I've also been adaptive snow skiing, and I've taken hot-air balloon rides with my kids. I've even flown in one of those acrobatic planes, duct taped to the seat. This is a great story! It happened in 2005. One of our Indy Lights drivers was sponsored by Klein Tools, which back then also sponsored a plane called a German A300. Well, I lucked into an invitation to take a ride one day and that was the only opening I needed. The challenge was to get me *in* the plane. Thankfully in the hangar they had a cherry picker that we rigged to raise me up over the plane and put me in the forward-facing rider location. That's when they brought out the duct tape to make sure my limbs wouldn't fly everywhere in the air. Little did I know the pilot's only goal for that day was to try and get me to throw up! He tried for forty-five minutes, but nothing worked. Eighth rolls, quarter rolls, half rolls, and every acrobatic trick he knew including flying upside down for over sixty seconds. What a blast. I remember being upside down in that plane just laughing.

I also raced a sailboat. When I found out that the US Paralympic sailing team was based in the St. Pete Harbor and wanted to let me try one of their boats, I jumped at the chance. Each boat held three people, and I'd have two people who had recently won a gold medal in the Olympics in China aboard with me! I was racing my friend Jim Guthrie. I sat in a fixed seat in the middle of my vessel, and I could steer using my chin. The goal was to race out by the St. Pete pier, go around a buoy, and come back. I remember thinking it looked a bit windy to be out on a small boat, but I figured that my teammates knew what they were doing. Well into the race, we were leading and everything was fantastic, until I heard from one of my crewmates, "Oh, s**t, we're in trouble." Not exactly something you want to hear from a gold medal winning sailor. He said the steering system broke. The next thing we knew, we'd passed the pier and the water was extremely choppy as we continued to float out to sea. We are seemingly on our way to Cuba! All I could think was I'd driven 240 miles per hour, and now I was going to die going 10 miles per hour in a sailboat. What seemed like an eternity later, the crew was able to get the boat working again and we finally turned around. It turned out the sailboat wasn't meant for water with more than ten knots of wind. That day? Fifteen knots. Guess I should have read the fine print.

Finally, let me tell you about my incredible skydiving experience. In 2021, my kids came up with the idea to jump out of a plane for Father's Day. I think they thought I'd balk at it, but instead, I said, "Why not?" I called my friend Matt Jaskol, who'd done several thousand jumps in his life, and he helped arrange everything. When you're in a wheelchair, every adventure takes a lot more planning, but not impossible. My biggest concern was the landing. Even though there was a soft pea-gravel area below, I kept thinking, *What if we miss*?

Once again, handy-dandy duct tape worked perfectly. We took motorcycle tie-downs and strapped my knees to my chest and then used duct tape to secure all of my limbs together. Then I was strapped onto my tandem instructor who was about 6′2″ and 250 pounds. We were the last ones to load into the plane before takeoff, which meant we also had to sit in the open doorway while the plane climbed to 12,000 feet. It seemed like that took forever—and it was freezing cold. When it was time to jump, I wasn't sure I was mentally ready to go. We reached a speed of 125 miles an hour on our descent before the parachute deployed. It was every bit as violent and exhilarating as I had imagined, and then some. It was an amazing feeling just floating in the air some 5,000 to 6,000 feet above the ground. It was crazy silent, yet you could hear everything from the ground. Then he said, "Let me show you what this parachute will do!" In my mind, we were doing just fine the way it was . . . But he proceeded to swerve back and forth in an effort to get us parallel with the ground, but it almost seemed upside down. No wonder people get hooked on this. Before I knew it, he was pirouetting and lining up for our landing. This is what I was most nervous about, but the guy did an incredible job and sacrificed himself so that my legs would be okay. It was even more special since I was able to do it with Savannah and Spencer as well as most of the team members from DRIVEN Las Vegas (talk about team bonding!).

I could go on and on for days about the many crazy things we have done as a team or as a family over the years. We are always figuring out creative ways to get me onto boats, helicopters, cruise ships, and pretty much anything so as not to miss out on a family activity. *Where there is a will, there's a way*—besides, what could go wrong? Break my neck? Been there, done that.

EPILOGUE

IN 2022, I was invited to share some of my hard-earned experience and give the keynote graduation speech at my alma mater, Pepperdine University in Malibu. I was also awarded an honorary doctorate, but that was far from the highlight of the day. The real honor was being there on stage as my son, Spencer, graduated on that very same day.

It can be difficult for me to get in front of a microphone. Not because I'm shy—far from it! Being paralyzed can make it hard to project my voice. Nevertheless, I agreed. Up there on stage in my ceremonial cap and gown, I talked to Spencer's class. I told them my mantra, "It's better to ask for forgiveness than for permission." But I also talked about how fulfilling it is for me to see others succeed. I congratulated them for getting through COVID and virtual learning. And I told them I was there that day thanks to the preparation Pepperdine gave me as a young person. I shared with them half a dozen lessons to help them get through life's journey. In summary, they are as follows:

1) Do not compromise your values—work hard and always do what you say you're going to do. Maintain your integrity.

2) Pick the right partner. I would not be alive today, let alone doing what I'm doing, if it wasn't for Sheila. Marriage is the single most important decision you will make in your life. Don't be stupid.
3) Follow your passion. Had I remained a healthcare administrator my life would have been totally different. And despite what happened on the racetrack, I don't regret following my passion.
4) You are not in control, God is. Everyone faces tragedy. You can't control that. It's about how you respond to what happens that makes you who you are.
5) Aim big and trust others. Success doesn't come alone, nor should it be sought solo. Strive for a better tomorrow and do it with those you love.
6) Believe in God's promise. Psalm 37 says, "Delight yourself in the Lord and He will give you the desires of your heart. Commit your way to the Lord, trust in Him, and he will act." I believe that. It's that faith that allowed me to dance with my daughter at her wedding and provides the belief that my body will be completely restored in Heaven.

With this advice in your back pocket, I told the graduating class at Pepperdine, you will go far. "I cannot tell you who to be, who to become, or what to do. But hopefully you can learn from my story. You can do the same from the great leaders of our world, all the alumni of this wonderful university, and from those you are blessed to have on your team." I concluded the address by saying, "Enjoy the process of the search without succumbing to the pressure of the result."

ACKNOWLEDGMENTS

Writing a book was always on my radar, but it was never a high priority. Then, as I approached my sixtieth birthday, I realized I was blessed to still be here and to still have both of my parents. I decided it was time to document their story and mine. It was a lengthy and educational process, and I am grateful to everyone who helped bring *No Finish Line* to life.

My overachieving daughter, Savannah, and our longtime friend Dr. Kimberly Meesters, an accomplished sports business leader, managed every aspect of the project, from finding a writer to pitching publishers to writing captions to editing the manuscript. We all quickly learned there is much more to publishing a book than just telling your story. Savannah, Kimberly, and I earned honorary editor titles after spending hours revising page after page. It felt like being back in college again, pulling all-nighters to meet a deadline. It was a great team effort!

Joe Verrengia from Arrow helped immensely with photos, Arrow approvals, and, of course, keeping me straight when it came to all the finer details. I really enjoyed reminiscing about all of our antics with the SAM car.

A special thank-you goes out to our friends at Indianapolis Motor Speedway for access to their robust photo archives and for their willingness to promote the book.

I also must say thanks to my friends and family who sat through interviews with Don Yaeger as he worked to help me make sense of all the memories. Don did a great job asking all the right questions and making everyone feel comfortable sharing their stories.

Scott Waxman was the first call we made when this was just a seed of an idea. He listened intently and offered valuable advice to help get this off the ground. Thank you to him and his team at Diversion for believing in this project and making it a reality.

Throughout this book, I have said racing is my passion and DRIVEN is my purpose. Many people have been instrumental in helping bring that purpose to life, but I owe a special thanks to Brandi Kurka. I can honestly say our original DRIVEN location in Las Vegas would not be a reality without her. She began as my personal assistant and worked her way up to executive director of DRIVEN. Now she has her most important job of all: mom!

Most of all, I appreciate *you* for reading. I am hopeful that my story inspires others to stay DRIVEN.